THE
LIVING
WORD

THE
LIVING
WORD

10 LIFE-CHANGING WAYS TO EXPERIENCE THE BIBLE

DOUGLAS D. WEBSTER

MOODY PUBLISHERS
CHICAGO

All Scripture quotations, unless otherwise indicated, are taken from the *Holy Bible, New International Version®*. NIV®. Copyright © 1973, 1978, 1984 by International Bible Society. Used by permission of Zondervan Publishing House. All rights reserved.

Scripture quotations marked NASB are taken from the *New American Standard Bible®*, Copyright © The Lockman Foundation 1960, 1962, 1963, 1968, 1971, 1972, 1973, 1975, 1977, 1995. Used by permission.

Scripture quotations marked NKJV are taken from the *New King James Version*. Copyright © 1982 by Thomas Nelson, Inc. Used by permission. All rights reserved.

Scripture quotations marked RSV are from the *Revised Standard Version* of the Bible, copyright 1946, 1952, and 1971 by the Division of Christian Education of the National Council of the Churches of Christ in the USA. Used by permission. All rights reserved.

Scripture quotations marked THE MESSAGE are from *The Message*, copyright © by Eugene H. Peterson 1993, 1994, 1995. Used by permission of NavPress Publishing Group.

Scripture quotations marked NEB are taken from *The New English Bible with the Apocrypha*. New York: Oxford University Press, © 1961, 1970 The Delegates of the Oxford University Press and The Syndics of the Cambridge University Press.

Scripture quotations marked KJV are taken from the King James Version.

Library of Congress Cataloging-in-Publication Data

Webster, Douglas D.
  The living Word : ten life-changing ways to experience the Bible /
Douglas D. Webster.
      p. cm.
    Includes bibliographical references.
    ISBN 0-8024-3017-1
    1. Word of God (Theology) 2. Christian life--Biblical teaching. I. Title.

  BT180.W67 W43 2003
  220--dc21

                                                    2002014848

                        1 3 5 7 9 10 8 6 4 2

Printed in the United States of America

To Paul and Merry Long
who live the Word they love

CONTENTS

1. Eat the Word   9
2. Meditate on the Word   21
3. Pray the Word   45
4. Model the Word   69
5. Picture the Word   89
6. Sing the Word   103
7. Study the Word   123
8. Preach the Word   155
9. Live the Word   179
10. Stay in the Word   201
     Notes   213

1

EAT
THE WORD

Lord, to whom shall we go? You have the words of eternal life.
We believe and know that you are the Holy One of God.

JOHN 6:68

*F*aith in the Lord Jesus is far more radical than we ever dreamed it would be. The Bible is a dangerous book because it leads us into a personal relationship with God. Those who limit faith to positive sentiments and good ideas soon find that God is far more than we bargained for. The Bible endangers our old way of living. It is not for everyone. The question is whether it is for you.

"This is a hard teaching. Who can accept it?"
(JOHN 6:60)

The crowd was open and receptive to Jesus' message until He applied the message personally: "I tell you the truth, unless you eat the flesh of the Son of Man and drink his blood, you have no life in you. Whoever eats my flesh and drinks my blood has eternal life, and I will raise him up at the last day" (vv. 53–54). This was too much for the people to stomach. The vivid analogy of eating dates back to the prophets Ezekiel and Jeremiah, who were commanded to eat God's revelation (Jeremiah 15:16; Ezekiel 2:8–3:3). The prophets were told to take in God's intelligible revelation as if it were food. They were to live on the Word of God, not guesswork. It was to become their very life. Eating God's revelation is the ultimate picture of personal participation. We cannot stand aloof or sit in judgment on the truth of God when we are eating it up!

THE GOOD BOOK

As long as we are talking about religion we can intellectualize the faith, but the moment we begin to take it in and absorb it into our blood stream we are transformed by it. There is a huge difference between an inspirational pep talk and the Gospel of Christ transforming every fiber of our being!

Some people like to think of the Bible as The Good Book—a religious resource that provides comfort and inspiration when you need it. Psalm 23 at funerals. 1 Corinthians 13 at weddings. Great stories for kids—like David and Goliath and Daniel in the lions' den. Thought-provoking advice for adults in Proverbs. Inspirational themes in the Psalms. Moral precepts in Jesus' parables. The Good Book is an aid in developing our own version of spirituality. It meets our felt needs. Many of us begin our spiritual journey with this kind of Bible.

There is an interesting parallel between what people feel they need spiritually and what Jesus gave the crowd physically. Felt needs range from the soul to the stomach; from emotional energy to physical strength. They were hungry, so Jesus miraculously fed them. He met a tangible, concrete physical need, but the need He met was meant to lead them to a deeper truth. The crowd read the miraculous sign as a pointer to the significance of Jesus, but they didn't know in what way He was significant. They were partly right— "Surely this is the Prophet who is to come into the world" (John 6:14)—but they imagined Jesus to be a political ruler. This is why they wanted to "come and make him king by force" (v. 15). Jesus slipped out of the performance trap and headed for the hills by Himself. The Good Book uses Jesus as a resource for inspiration and emotional uplift, but Jesus expects more. He said it boldly, "Whoever eats my flesh and drinks my blood remains in me, and I in him. Just as the living Father sent me and I live because of the Father, so the one who feeds on me will live because of me" (vv. 56–57).

THE HOLY BIBLE

Others go beyond the spirituality of The Good Book to the religion of The Holy Bible. They believe in the sacred importance of religious tradition. The Bible is more than a guide for personal spirituality. It represents a tradition that is larger than the individual self and an institution that extends from antiquity to modernity. The Holy Bible becomes an icon to them, symbolizing the Christian tradition. Jesus addressed this perspective when He confronted the Pharisees. "You diligently study the Scriptures because you think that by them you possess eternal life. These are the Scriptures that testify about me, yet you refuse to come to me to have life" (John 5:39–40). It is ironic that The Holy Bible should become a possession that prevents a personal relationship with the Lord Jesus Christ.

When I was a senior in high school, I visited a Christian college with a good friend of mine to see if I should apply to the college. We visited a sociology class on the day that the professor was trying to demystify the aura surrounding the Bible. He surprised us all when he took his Bible and threw

Jesus led the people beyond their physical felt needs to their need for God.

it on the floor and began to jump on it. His point was that the Bible is not an object of worship but a witness to truth. He wanted us to know that there was nothing holy about the pages and the binding. I'm not sure the students understood what he was trying to say. My friend surely didn't understand his point about the Bible. He thought the professor must be crazy. His only comment was, "You sure don't want to go to this college!"

Religious leaders, both in Jesus' day and our

own, focus on the Bible as an object of study and debate, but they miss the true message of the Word of God. The Holy Bible becomes an end in itself. It does not lead its preachers, scholars, teachers, and Bible study leaders to Christ, but to one another's opinions about the Bible.

Jesus led the people beyond their physical felt needs to their need for God. "Do not work for food that spoils, but for food that endures to eternal life, which the Son of Man will give you. On him, God the Father has placed his seal of approval" (John 6:27). Jesus was effective in drawing the connection between obvious physical needs and the greater need for God. But people clung to their religious tradition and debated the deeper truth of God. They wanted a sign. They wanted proof. Not an unreasonable expectation when you consider human nature and how prone we are to deception and gullibility. But Jesus challenged them to see Himself as the fulfillment of the Word of God. He took them further than sentiment or tradition could possibly

Jesus' reliance upon the Father to draw people to Himself did not remove the scandal of faith.

go. "The work of God is this: to believe in the one he has sent. . . . For the bread of God is he who comes down from heaven and gives life to the world. . . . I am the bread of life" (vv. 29, 33, 35). No one could arrive at this conclusion with just the sentiment of The Good Book or merely possessing The Holy Bible.

Jesus knew the weakness of human sentiment, logic, and tradition, and that is why He said, "All that the Father gives me will come to me, and whoever comes to me I will never drive away" (v. 37). When the people imposed their limited understanding on Him ("Is this not Jesus, the son of Joseph, whose father and mother we know? How can he now say, 'I came down from heaven'?" v. 42), He responded, "Stop grumbling among yourselves. . . . No one can come to me unless the Father who sent me draws him, and I will raise him up at the last day" (vv. 43–44).

Jesus' reliance upon the Father to draw people to Himself did not remove the scandal of faith. It did not stop people from intellectualizing His message. It did not stop people from arguing sharply among themselves and framing questions in ways that made Jesus seem foolish, such as, "How can this man give us his flesh to eat?" (v. 52). On the contrary, Jesus' reliance on the Father caused Him to intensify the scandal of faith. "I tell you the truth, unless you eat the flesh of the Son of Man and drink his blood, you have no life in you" (v. 53).

The so-called disciples who prefer the spiritual sentiment of The Good Book and possess the religious tradition of The Holy Bible are almost forced to conclude pessimistically, "This is a hard teaching. Who can accept it?" Instead of confessing Christ, they end up grumbling. Churches are filled with self-centered spiritual people of The Good Book and religious people of The Holy Bible, who grumble and complain. The Good Book people look for empathy and excitement; The Holy Bible people look for tradition and status. But both miss out on Jesus. On hearing the message they say, "This is a hard teaching. Who can accept it?" They can't swallow the real truth about Jesus.

"Does this offend you?" (JOHN 6:61)

It is remarkable that Jesus, the Living Word, should have to ask, "Does this offend you?" The very One who laid down His life for our salvation is judged offensive. Many today are looking for empathy, but not to the degree or depth offered by God. They will listen to people who share their questions and identify with their struggles. But the One who identified with us in our need by going to the Cross and dying for our sins is forgotten. People prefer the shared pathos of fellow sufferers to Christ's passion for

The source for salvation and spirituality does not lie in ourselves.

them. It is true that we are no longer impressed by external authorities who tell us what to believe. Rick Richardson has wisely observed, "In the past, being an expert and having the answers were what built credibility and a hearing. Today, having the same questions, struggles and hurts is what builds credibility and gains a hearing."[1]

The difficulty, however, is that people have trouble going beyond the shared pathos of suffering and skepticism to believing that God identifies with their suffering and offers salvation from their sin. But this is exactly what God has provided for us. In Christ, God's identification with us in our need is complete. "The Word became flesh and [lived for a while] among us"

(John 1:14). Yet there is more, much more, to Jesus than empathy. The apostle John adds, "We have seen his glory, the glory of the One and Only [Son], who came from the Father, full of grace and truth." Christ not only identifies with us in our need but saves us completely.

Wherein lies the offense? Does it lie in the fact that faith in Jesus is all-consuming: "Unless you eat the flesh of the Son of Man and drink his blood"? Is it that God's love and glory transcends our sin and suffering? Jesus called for an enlarged vision: "What if you see the Son of Man ascend to where he was before!" (John 6:62). Beyond the sentiment of The Good Book and the religion of The Holy Book stands the crucified Lord of Glory, the Living Word. Jesus invites us to enlarge our vision and embrace God's grace. What is certain is that the source for salvation and spirituality does not lie in ourselves. It is not a question of our willpower. Even the choice for God is a gift of God's grace. As Jesus reiterated, "This is why I told you that no one can come to me unless the Father has enabled him" (v. 65).

"Lord, to whom shall we go?" (JOHN 6:68)

How shall we weigh Peter's response? Is he trapped and forced to toe the party line? Perhaps that's what the skeptic thinks, but the follower of Jesus knows otherwise. Peter speaks as one whose heart has been set free. Peter is not manipulated—he is liberated. His confession is emphatic: "You have the words of eternal life. We believe and know that you are the Holy One of God" (v. 69). The bond of marriage knows the exclusivity of this oneness; the groom and bride feel no limitation in vowing, "You are the one!" Similarly, yet on an altogether higher plane, the bond of faith knows the freedom and peace of this confession, "You have the words of eternal life." Peter's confession reminds us of the man in Jesus' parable who discovered a treasure hidden in a field. He sold everything he had and bought the field. Peter is like the merchant who finally found the perfect pearl and sold everything he had to buy it (Matthew 13:44–46). In the Spirit, Peter has discovered the Way, the Truth, and the Life (see John 14:6).

Do you share Peter's response? In this passage there were only two reactions to Jesus: Those who said, "This is a hard saying. Who can accept it?" and Peter, who appears to speak for the Twelve, when he confesses, "We believe and know that you are the Holy One of God" (6:69). John tells us that at this point many of His disciples turned back and no longer followed Jesus (v. 66). Only a few are willing to take in the Living Word.

Jesus' question to the disciples is an important question for us today. What would you say if Jesus asked you, "You do not want to leave, too, do you?"

Does Peter speak for you? "Lord, to whom shall we go? You have the words of eternal life. We believe and know that you are the Holy One of God."

2

MEDITATE ON THE WORD

I have hidden your word in my heart that I might not sin against you. . . . I meditate on your precepts and consider your ways. I delight in your decrees; I will not neglect your word.

PSALM 119:11, 15–16

I have only a vague notion of why I started reading my Bible every morning. I was in my early teens and it seemed like something Christians should do. We read the Bible as a family and it seemed important for me to begin reading it for myself. I don't remember my parents saying, "You should read your Bible more," but they might have. In any case, I got into the habit and it quickly became part of my life. I got up thirty minutes earlier than I had to for school and read my Bible at my desk in my bedroom. I had a quiet room and a good desk, two practical things that aided my daily devotions. Setting aside a particular place for a time of quiet meditation on the Word encouraged me in this spiritual discipline.

After a brief prayer for guidance, I started into the passage for the day. I rarely used a commentary or study guide, preferring to use just the Bible. I read through biblical books, balancing my reading between the Old and New Testaments. A comment by Stuart Briscoe, a pastor in Milwaukee, stayed with me through the years. He suggested that in our daily Bible reading we should read until we are struck by a truth that calls for deeper consideration and reflection. Invariably something in the biblical text stood out to me and caused me to think about my relationship to Christ or made me wonder why God worked the way He did. I was free with my questioning and doubts, but I was also open to receive God's direction and take it to heart.

I kept a journal. I wrote down my questions, observations, doubts, and reflections on a daily loose-leaf calendar. I saved these notes for a number of years in a shoe box, but never went back to read them. Writing my thoughts, feelings, and questions in response to the Word of

God was a valuable spiritual exercise for me. It helped me to focus my mind on Christ and to articulate what I was thinking and feeling. I concluded my time in the Word with prayer.

This simple routine of daily Bible reading and prayer has done far more to shape my life in Christ than anything else I've done. I am convinced that without this spiritual discipline all my formal theological training would have been of little benefit.

Meditating on the Word of God in the morning is a daily reminder of first things first.

Meditating on the Word helped me to internalize God's truth and process my life experiences. It made me much more conscious of God's work in others and God's will for my life. The daily morning discipline of being in the Word and in the Spirit for the sake of our heart's devotion and our life's salvation is invaluable.

IN THE MORNING

Dietrich Bonhoeffer, the well-known German pastor and martyr, was a strong advocate for morning meditation and prayer. He reasoned that since Jesus rose "very early in the morning" and "went off to a solitary place" to pray, so should we (Mark 1:35). Bonhoeffer insisted that our first thoughts should not be "our own plans and worries, not even for our zeal to accomplish our own work, but for God's liberating grace, God's sanctifying presence. . . . Before our daily bread should be the daily Word. Only thus will the bread be received with thanksgiving. Before our daily work should be the morning prayer. Only thus will the work be done as the fulfillment of God's command. The morning must yield an hour of quiet time for prayer and common devotion. That is certainly not wasted time. How else could we prepare ourselves to face the tasks, cares, and temptations of the day?"[1]

For the psalmist, the morning is a special time to meet God. "In the morning, O LORD, you hear my voice; in the morning I lay my requests before you and wait in expectation" (Psalm 5:3). Meditating on the Word of God in the morning is a daily reminder of first things first. Bonhoeffer's almost lyrical description of the value of meeting with God in the morning cannot be dismissed lightly.

Each morning is a new beginning of our life. Each day is a finished whole. The present day marks the boundary of our cares and concerns (Matt. 6:34; James 4:14). It is long enough to find God or to lose him, to keep faith or fall into disgrace. God created day and night for us so we need not wander without boundaries, but may be able to see every morning the goal of the evening ahead. Just as the ancient sun rises anew every day, so the eternal mercy of God is new every morning (Lam. 3:23). Every morning God gives us the gift of comprehending anew his faithfulness of old; thus, in the midst of our life with God, we may daily begin a new life with him. . . . Before the heart unlocks itself for the world, God wants to open it for himself; before the ear takes in the countless voices of the day, it should hear in the early hours the voice of the Creator and Redeemer. God prepared the stillness of the first morning for himself. It should remain his.[2]

IN THE WORD

We begin the day by listening to God's Word. Meditation provides the opportunity to obey the admonition, "Let the word of Christ dwell in you richly" (Colossians 3:16). It is a means by which we "humbly accept" the implanted Word (James 1:21). Meditation is not a luxury we do for ourselves to clear our heads for the coming rush of daily activities. Our focus is not on our feelings or moods, but on the concrete, defining, sure Word of God. It is an act of obedience. It is not a device for assuring tranquility or inspiring success. True meditation does not domesticate the Word of the Lord, but causes us to truly hear the voice of God. At times the Word will lead us "beside quiet waters." It will restore our souls and guide us in paths of righteousness (Psalm 23:2–3), but at other times it will be a fire in our bones (Jeremiah 20:9) demanding immediate action. It will be like a hammer shattering the rock of sinful pride and complacency (23:29). Some mornings the impact of the Word of God will be so great that it will feel like we've been handling dynamite.

I remember one such morning. I was reading in Luke: "If anyone would come after me, he must deny himself and take up his cross daily and follow me. For whoever wants to save his life will lose it, but whoever loses his life for me will save it" (Luke 9:23–24). I was a senior at Wheaton College at the time and working on plans for the coming year. On that particular morning, after devotions I had planned to write to Dr. Paul Han in Taiwan, who had invited me to teach at Chun Yuan Christian College in the fall. I had it all worked out in my mind that I would go to Taiwan not in September, as he requested, but in December. I wanted to

True meditation is not done alone but in dialogue with God.

spend the first semester working on my master's degree, but even more than that I wanted to spend time with Ginny. I was in love, and I couldn't imagine being apart most of the summer and then flying off to Taiwan to teach for a year. I knew exactly what I wanted to say to Dr. Han. I would thank him for his gracious invitation and tell him that I couldn't come in the fall but I'd be able to come for the second semester.

The only obstacle that morning to *dictating* to the Lord and Dr. Han *my terms* of commitment was the Word of God. There I was, innocently reading about taking up my cross and following Jesus. I was naively reflecting on those who so easily excused themselves from following Jesus, "I will follow you, Lord, but . . . ," when suddenly it hit me that I was about to do the same thing! Of course, Dr. Han wanted me in the fall—that's when teachers start the school year. I had prayed so much that the Lord would work out this opportunity and lead Dr. Han, and yet when it came down to accepting the assignment I was ready to handle the situation on my own, according to my own agenda. I will never forget that morning because the meaning of the Word struck me with such force. I immediately wrote to Dr. Han saying I would be there at the time he requested.

Through prayerful meditation we internalize the Word of God. We not only take it seriously, we engage it personally. We ask what God is saying to us in this particular text. We realize that our natural, sinful tendency is to override the voice of God, but meditation on the Word disrupts that incessant selfish monologue. When we begin each morning asking the Lord to speak to us from His Word we are asking for far more than we imagined. We are opening up a dialogue with God that will challenge every sin, bias, prejudice, and habit—that is, *everything* that lies outside of God's will. We are also opening ourselves up to the comfort of our heavenly Father, whose Word brings peace and joy. Above all else it is our desire to hear the voice of God, and the only way to hear His voice is to be in the Spirit.

IN THE SPIRIT

Being in the Word and being in the Spirit are essentially one and the same. We cannot have one without the other. Discernment depends on the Spirit of God opening up our hearts and minds to the Word of God. "We have not received the spirit of the world," said the apostle Paul, "but the Spirit who is from God, that we may understand what God has freely given us. . . . The [person] without the Spirit does not accept the things that come from the Spirit of God" (1 Corinthians 2:12, 14). The purpose of the Spirit of truth is to guide us "into all truth" (John 16:13). Meditating on the Word of God is not an independent exercise performed in solo. True meditation is not done alone but in dialogue with God. "This is the very reason why we begin our meditation with the prayer that God may send His Holy Spirit to us through His Word and reveal His Word to us and enlighten us."[3]

Jesus stated the purpose of the Spirit this way: "He will not speak on his own; he will speak only what he hears, and he will tell you what is yet to come. He will bring glory to me by taking from what is mine and making it known to you" (John 16:13–14). Apart from the Spirit of Christ, we may study the Bible as an ancient text, but we do not hear the voice of God. J. I. Packer defines meditation as "an activity of holy thought, consciously performed in the presence of God, under the eye of God, by the help of God, as a means of communion with God."[4] The illuminating presence and revealing perspective of the Spirit of God is crucial to hearing the Word of God. Like the apostle John, we need to see our life circumstances in the light of "the word of God and the testimony of Jesus." If we expect to hear the voice of God, we will need to be "in the Spirit" (Revelation 1:9–10).

Depend upon this daily feeding on God's Word for comfort, correction, guidance, and instruction.

Because of the Spirit of God, meditating on the Word is not a private experience. Even our meditative thoughts and feelings are not our own, but are developed in close communion with God. Many think of meditation as a private experience, but we are not left alone to interpret the Scriptures on our own. This is why Peter insisted that we understand "that no prophecy of Scripture came about by the prophet's own interpretation. For prophecy never had its origin in the will of man, but men spoke from God as they were carried along by the Holy Spirit" (2 Peter 1:20–21). What was true in the giving of Scripture is also true in the receiving of Scripture. Neither the origin nor the interpretation of the Word of God is left to the human will. Just as the prophets "spoke from God as they were carried along by the Holy Spirit," so we need to hear from God as we are carried along by the Holy Spirit.

IN MY HEART

Meditation was never meant to be a private experience, in the sense of being alone with one's self, independent of God. It was always meant to be a deeply personal experience. Morning meditation on the Word of God, in the Spirit, opens our hearts to the truth and wisdom of God. This is why many believers call their personal time of Bible study and prayer their devotional time. They take in the Word as an act of heartfelt devotion to

God. It is much more than a mental exercise or a spiritual discipline. They love to hear the voice of God in His Word, and they depend upon this daily feeding on God's Word for comfort, correction, guidance, and instruction.

Since meditation involves being alone with God, it has a way of revealing the heart's desire. Intelligent people can sound knowledgeable about God and emotional people can sound passionate about God, but people who spend time alone with God and His Word *know* that they have been with God. Instead of a knowledge *about* God they have a knowledge *of* God. Through the prophets, the Lord lamented the emptiness of the people's religion. "These people come near to me with their mouth and honor me with their lips, but their hearts are far from me" (Isaiah 29:13). The Lord looked forward to the day when He would establish a new covenant. External religion would be replaced by internal devotion to God. The Lord de-

If we hide God's Word in our heart it will be evident in everything we do!

clared, "I will put my law in their minds and write it on their hearts" (Jeremiah 31:33).

Hearing the Word of God with our heart is no excuse for eliminating the mind. All that is required for an intelligent, thoughtful reading of the text is assumed in a heartfelt hearing of the Word of God. But to hear the Word in my heart is to take it in personally. Instead of simply stating the truth, I identify with the truth. I own it, celebrate it, and cherish it! In the deepest part of me, I say, "Amen!" to God's Word. I resonate with the message and take delight in God's Word. I feel like the psalmist when he said, "The precepts of the LORD are right, giving joy to the heart. . . . They are more precious than gold, than much pure gold; they are sweeter than honey, than honey from the comb" (Psalm 19:8, 10). To open the Word of God is to open our whole being to the will of God, from our innermost self to every aspect of our lives. If we hide God's Word in our heart it will be evident in everything we do!

Those who hold God's Word in their heart emphasize the value of memorizing special verses that bring comfort, challenge, and concentration upon God's truth. A friend of mine is going through a very difficult time in her marriage. She has turned to Scripture memory to focus her mind on God's promises and to remind herself of the Lord's abiding presence. This comfort did not happen overnight, but as she memorized God's Word she found herself recalling these verses, sometimes in the middle of the night when she could not sleep. Knowing these verses by heart often led her to prayer and to a sense of God's peace.

I know that the Psalms have taken on a deeper meaning for me since I began to memorize several verses each week for the Sunday morning call to worship. When I memorize a biblical passage, I usually type it and print several copies. I put a copy on the dashboard of my car and often carry another copy with me as I do my workout. I have found that focusing on the ideas of the passage rather than word-for-word memorization has helped me retain the verse easier.

Our children's ministry program at church has focused on Scripture memory for some time, and the benefits are evident. Key truths are not only taught but memorized. Even young children feel like they are part of our Sunday morning worship experience. When we pray the Lord's Prayer, I hear the children praying right along with the adults.

Memorizing God's Word strengthens our grasp of the whole counsel of God's Word. Ginny, my wife, has an excellent recall of biblical truth, which I attribute to years of Bible reading and memorization. Growing up in Brazil in a missionary boarding school where Scripture memorization was encouraged but not imposed, instilled within her a love for the Word of God. Memorization never became an end in itself and it was never used to show off Bible knowledge, but it cultivated within her a lifelong desire to understand God's perspective on life's experiences. Through memorization Ginny learned how to meditate on God's Word.

IN MY LIFE

Let's take Psalm 84 as a focus for personal meditation. Begin with prayer, asking God to open His Word to you and send His Spirit to illuminate the meaning and the emotion of this psalm. What is the first thing that impresses you about this psalm? It is easy to see why Derek Kidner writes, "Longing is written all over this psalm."[5] The psalmist causes us to reflect on our passion for the presence of God. Can we share his emotion for God? From the first line, every praise note is an exclamation from the heart. "How lovely is your dwelling place, O LORD Almighty!" With his whole being, he cries out for God. "My soul yearns, even faints, for the courts of the LORD; my heart and my flesh cry out for the living God" (v. 2). There is a huge difference between the "I," "me," and "my" of self-centered existence and the deeply personal devotion to God expressed in this psalm.

To meditate on this psalm is to ask whether my soul really yearns for God. Does my heart ache for the presence of God? There are any number of reasons why this longing for God is rare in our culture, even in the church, but instead of generalizing the reasons for this, personalize the issue. Do I share the psalmist's yearning for the reality of God? Is my heart's desire for God different from the psalmist's? If so, why? Is there anything that hinders my passion for Christ? How do I express my need for God?

We can understand the Little Leaguer's thrill at getting a base hit or the father's happiness over a hug from his daughter, but can we feel what the psalmist felt about the Lord? We can identify with the business person's joy over a promotion or a college student's pride at graduation, but can we say, "My heart and my flesh cry out for the living God"?

The psalmist used concrete, practical language for experiencing the presence of God. Terms such as *dwelling place, the courts of the* LORD, and *house* convey a definite sense of place. These words were not meant to limit God to the tabernacle or the temple, but to affirm the reality of God's presence. This psalm is not about finding God

Above all else, the psalmist wants to be at home with God.

in a "sacred place," but about experiencing God in *our* time and space. This psalm is not about attending church, supporting programs, or serving on committees. It is about knowing God in the fellowship of God's people. The terms *home* and *nest* emphasize both intimacy and community. Any hint of a solitary, private religious experience is dismissed by the psalmist's keen sense of a robust fellowship of faithful worshipers. "Blessed are those who dwell in your house; they are ever praising you" (v. 4). The psalmist knows the difference between spiritual infatuation and

God-centered concentration. He is responding to the altar call of his heart. He is "envious" of the sparrow who has found a home, "a place near your altar, O LORD Almighty, my King and my God" (v. 3).

Above all else, the psalmist wants to be at home with God. How does this compare to my sense of being at home with God? For me, it conveys the important truth that *home is not where I'm from but where I'm going.* Knowing God is my life theme, and *the measure of my life is not in what I achieve for myself, but in what I receive from the Lord.*

To meditate on this psalm is to ask a personal question: How have I experienced the meaning and significance of life? Has it come primarily through personal achievement and self-effort, or by God's gracious gift? This psalm reminds me that my little life story—including my hometown, my immediate family, my childhood experiences, my education, my work, my wife, my children, and all those experiences that I use to describe where I have been and where I'm going—remain truly insignificant apart from God's great salvation history story. It is God's saving, sanctifying work in my life that infuses meaning and significance for me. The psalmist's longing for God helps me see that *everyone has a story but only His story redeems our story.*

Prayerful meditation draws a crucial connection between the psalmist's longing for the "dwelling place" of God and the truth of the Incarnation of God. The apostle John used this same concrete language of time and place to express the presence of God in Christ. "The Word became flesh and made his dwelling among us. We have seen his glory, the glory of the One and Only, who came from the Father, full of grace and truth" (John 1:14). The language of God's "dwelling" with us and of our "abiding" in Christ (15:4 KJV) focuses and intensifies the language of the psalms.

The more we thirst for God, the more refreshing we are to others.

The apostle Paul brought this imagery home in the most personal way possible when he said, "Don't you know that you yourselves are God's temple and that God's Spirit lives in you? . . . Do you not know that your body is a temple of the Holy Spirit, who is in you, whom you have received from God?" (1 Corinthians 3:16; 6:19).

Today, we listen to the psalmist's longing for the presence of God with a deep awareness of God's gracious and loving effort to overcome the distance that separates us from Him. God has come to us. "Here I am! I stand at the door and knock. If anyone hears my voice and opens the door, I will come in and eat with him, and he with me" (Revelation 3:20).

At the heart of Psalm 84, the theme changes from the longing for the presence of God to the experience of the pilgrimage to God. The psalmist knows he is not at home yet. "Blessed are those whose strength is in you, who have set their hearts on pilgrimage" (v. 5). The paradox of peace and pilgrimage, rest and restlessness runs through this psalm. On the one hand, "even the sparrow has found a home," and on the other, "they go from strength to strength, till each appears before God in Zion" (vv. 3, 7). To yearn for the courts of the Lord is to set out on a life journey toward God. This psalm prompts me to ask, "Have I truly set my heart on pilgrimage, or am I too busy living for selfish pursuits?" Those who have "set their hearts on pilgrimage" pass through the Baca Valley, a place which symbolizes the hardships of the journey. The singular

Baca, translated "balsam trees" or "aspens," refers to a tree or shrub that grows in arid places. Those who pass through "the thirsty valley" (NEB) "make it a place of springs." They "dare to dig blessings out of hardships."[6]

To meditate on this psalm is to ask how God has worked in my life to transform the arid, parched earth of suffering and sorrow, pain and disappointment, into a place of worship and friendship fed by the living water of Christ. How has the desert of despair turned into springs of everlasting life? The psalmist sees life, not as a survivor weathering one crisis after another, but as an explorer or a challenger going from strength to strength. The psalmist's tone is confident; his perspective is realistic. There is hope for the journey home. "They go from strength to strength till each appears before God in Zion" (v. 7). The more faith in God is exercised, the stronger it grows. The more dependent we are upon God, the more dependable we become. The more we thirst for God, the more refreshing we are to others. The apostle Paul expressed this same theme when he said, "I press on toward the goal to win the prize for which God has called me heavenward in Christ

Jesus" (Philippians 3:14). *Remember—home is not where we're from but where we're going.*

Meditation draws out the source of the psalmist's confidence. This is God-centered confidence. Those who go from strength to strength depend exclusively on God. They cry out, "Hear my prayer, O LORD God Almighty; listen to me, O God of Jacob" (Psalm 84:8). Those who seek the presence of God find the source of their strength in God. I am led to ask, "Given today's challenges, how can I depend upon the Lord? What am I up against that *requires* me to turn to God for wisdom and help?" Questions such as these transform daily devotions into a *necessity* if we expect to go from strength to strength.

The psalmist concludes by stressing two things. First, he reminds us of his longing for the presence of God. Second, he states the profound truth that underlies everything that has been prayed in the psalm, that is, the complete sufficiency and unsurpassed goodness of God.

His longing for God is highlighted by drawing two comparisons. "Better is one day in your courts than a thousand elsewhere; I would rather be a doorkeeper in the house of my God than dwell in the tents of the wicked" (v. 10). In other words, there is nothing that compares in joy or value to the presence of God. How can I express this in my own words? Can I say with the psalmist that I'd rather be a brother in the Household of Faith than a CEO of a major corporation? Or, that I'd rather be a servant of Christ than sailing a forty-foot yacht? The psalm asks me to evaluate my life goals, to take stock of my personal ambition, and to reflect on that which is most significant to me.

Psalm 84 ends as it began—with the goodness of God. There is nothing heavy or belabored about the psalmist's spirituality. There is nothing here that hints of a languid, cheerless piety. He does not turn prayer and praise into self-expression, nor does he use God to put himself on display. He closes with a benediction of praise. "For the LORD God is a sun and shield" (v. 11). With two simple metaphors, the psalmist deftly captures the range of God's wonderful attributes. The sun stands for all that is positive—the light, joy, heat, and energy that radiates from God. The shield symbolizes all that is protective about God's sovereign strength and might. I hold to this assurance: "No good thing does he withhold from those whose walk is blameless" (v. 11). My heart concludes, "O LORD

Almighty, blessed is the [person] who trusts in you" (v. 12). My morning meditation in the Word, in the Spirit, opens my heart and my life to the presence of God—to the voice of God.

3

PRAY
THE WORD

I keep asking that the God of our Lord Jesus Christ,
the glorious Father, may give you the Spirit of wisdom
and revelation, so that you may know him better.

EPHESIANS 1:17

*T*he first picture of prayer that we have in
the Psalms, the Bible's Book of Prayer, is
of a person who delights in the Word of the Lord,
"and on his law he meditates day and night"
(Psalm 1:2). This is a reminder that all prayer is
rooted in the Word of God, because all prayer is a
response to what God has said. The apostle Paul's
admonition to pray continually (1 Thessalonians
5:17) is fulfilled in the psalmist's picture of meditating on the Word constantly. People can read
the Bible academically, study it linguistically, follow it morally, appreciate it artistically, and enjoy

it emotionally, but until they are moved to respond to God in prayer they haven't really heard the Word of God. To truly hear the Word of God is to hear it prayerfully, or not at all.

Prayer is best understood as answering the God who speaks to us through His Word. It is hard to imagine that anyone who has heard the voice of God would give Him the silent treatment. It is equally unimaginable that anyone would persist in speaking to God and then refuse to hear what the Lord has to say. But many who claim to know the Bible seldom pray, and those who do pray often see little connection between their prayers and the Bible. In the absence of the Word, prayer becomes a kind of spiritual monologue carried along by emotion or ritual. But in dialogue with the Word, prayer becomes communion with God.

It is possible to study the Bible for years but never internalize the message through prayer. Is this not why Jesus repeatedly said, "He who has ears, hear let him hear" (Matthew 11:15)? In his book *Deceived by God? A Journey Through Suffering,* theologian John Feinberg honestly admits that his extensive study of the problem of evil did little to comfort him when his wife, Patricia, was diagnosed with Huntington's Disease, a genetically transmitted disease that involves the premature deterioration of the brain. In seminary, Feinberg wrote his master of divinity thesis on Job. Later, he devoted his master of theology thesis to God's sovereignty and human freedom.

Prayer is best understood as answering the God who speaks to us through His Word.

Still absorbed in the problem of evil, he focused his doctoral dissertation on the subject.

Yet after all of those years of serious biblical and theological study he felt as though he had no perspective to help him deal with the devastating reality of his wife's life-threatening illness. All of his intellectual work had missed his soul. "The truth is," Feinberg admits, "I couldn't figure it out. I had all those intellectual answers, but none of them made any difference in how I felt on the personal level. As a professor of theology, surely I should understand what God was doing in this situation. On the contrary, I began wondering if in fact I really understood anything at all about God. The emotional and psychological pain was unrelenting, and even devastating physical pain resulted from the stress. . . . I was experiencing a religious crisis, and none of this information I had stored away seemed to matter in the least."[1]

What makes Feinberg's book on pain especially worthwhile is that he has the courage to contrast his own spiritual helplessness with his wife's deeply internalized faith. Patricia describes her initial reaction to the bad news: "I was extremely shocked when this disease was diagnosed. I *knew* that when physical problems come, one should thank God for his presence and strength in the midst of those problems, rather than becoming bitter. And I *knew* that I should do that whether I felt like it or not; so that's what I did on the way home in the car. I also *knew* 1 Thessalonians 5:18, which says, 'Give thanks in all circumstances, for this is God's will for you in Christ Jesus.' No matter what the circumstances, God is still there, and he is in control of all that happens. He is faithful to his Word. That is *reason* for thanksgiving, and I continue to thank him each day."[2]

> *Hearing the Word and prayer are inseparable. Taken together they mark our agreement with God's will.*

One of the first things that Patricia did was to read through the Psalms and write down every reference "having to do with God's strength in time of trouble." Psalm 46:1 was especially comforting: "God is our refuge and strength, an ever-present help in trouble." Through prayer, Patricia was able to hear the Word of God in her pain. "God made that verse true in my life. I have confidence in his presence, even in the midst of this disease."[3]

Instead of reading the Bible for intellectual ideas on the subject of suffering, she prayerfully read the Bible as personal guidance for living with God and for God through pain and suffering. When Patricia read in Romans 9:20, "But who are you, O man, to talk back to God? Shall what is formed say to him who formed it, 'Why did you make me like this?'" she humbly concluded, "God has the right to do anything he wants with me. Who am I to complain?"

She took to heart the apostle Paul's doxology, "Praise be to the God and Father of our Lord Jesus Christ, the Father of compassion and the God of all comfort, who comforts us in all our troubles, so that we can comfort those in any trouble with the comfort we ourselves have received from

God" (2 Corinthians 1:3–4). Instead of being crushed by her terminal illness, she testified, "The Lord has given me such complete comfort that I wanted to find ways to share it with others."[4]

Hearing the Word and prayer are inseparable. Taken together they mark our agreement with God's will. They signal our partnership with God. Through prayer we are given the opportunity of agreeing with the living God. The Lord certainly doesn't need our approval, but He invites, even desires, our participation in His creative, redeeming work. "Everything God created is good," wrote the apostle Paul, provided "it is received with thanksgiving, because it is consecrated by *the word of God and prayer*" (1 Timothy 4:4–5, italics added).

Prayer is always the catalyst for action in Jesus' life.

Prayer is absolutely crucial for hearing the Word, as Paul reminds us in his letter to the Philippians. "This is my prayer," he writes: "that your love may abound more and more in knowledge and depth of insight, so that you may be able to discern what is best and may be pure and blameless until the day of Christ, filled with the fruit of righteousness that comes through Jesus Christ—to the glory and praise of God" (Philippians 1:9–11). Paul has given us an example of how we can pray for one another and for ourselves. Hearing the Word and prayer go hand in hand. What Jesus said of marriage applies to the Word and prayer, "What God has joined together, let [no one] separate" (Matthew 19:6).

THE WORD ON PRAYER

Before we hear the Word prayerfully we need to hear how prayer works in the Word. One of the first things we discover is that prayer is at the center of what God is doing. From the Garden of Eden to the island of Patmos, prayer plots the course of God's salvation history story. The interchange between God and His people is recorded through prayer. If we were to take out the prayers and edit the Bible of all dialogue between God and man, we wouldn't have much of a Word to hear! What is true for the Bible is also true for us. If prayer were removed from our lives and nothing changed, it would be a definite indicator that we were not listening to God.

Abraham answered God's call with prayers in

the wilderness and wrestled with the promises of God in prayer. God began a dialogue with Moses over a burning bush and with the Exodus inspired Moses to pray songs of praise. Prayer is at the center of Joshua's battle at Jericho, Gideon's strategy with the Midianites, Naomi's return to Bethlehem, and Hannah's dedication of Samuel. David is neither priest nor prophet, but his life is best understood as a life of prayer. From Elijah on, the prophets are an in-depth study of prayer. How could we tell the stories of Isaiah, Jeremiah, and Ezekiel apart from their prayers? The true stories of Jonah and Habakkuk are testimonies of how prayer changes lives.

The prayers of the Bible show us how God's people received His Word. Such prayers do not impress us as decorative speech or pious talk, but as honest, straight-from-the-heart responses to God. News of the Incarnation inspired prayer, as attested to in Mary's praise, Zechariah's song, and Simeon's benediction. Prayer is always the catalyst for action in Jesus' life. It precipitates the confrontation in the wilderness and the initiative that leads to the calling of the disciples. In the Gospels, we sense the immediacy of Jesus' dialogue with the Father, His freedom from all pretense and ritual. Prayer sets the whole tenor of His ministry from the boy who must be in His Father's house (Luke 2:49) to the man who called out with a loud voice, "Father, into your hands I commit my spirit" (23:46).

Jesus guides us in how we should pray. He condemned the performance prayers of "hypocrites" (Matthew 6:5), who loved to be seen in public praying. He was intent on stripping away all forms of artificiality and false piety from prayer. "When you pray, do not keep on babbling like pagans, for they think they will be heard because of their many words" (v. 7). His example of prayer strikes us with its simplicity and scope.

Real prayer is our response to God's initiative; it is our dialogue with His revelation.

We are reminded that all true prayer issues out of the body of Christ, the community of God's people, and is direct address: "Our Father in heaven, hallowed be your name, your kingdom come, your will be done on earth as it is in heaven" (vv. 9–10).

There is nothing new in this line that has not been prayed a thousand times in the Psalms. Jesus did not feel the compulsion to discuss the obvious limits of language to communicate the full reality of God. He did not feel the need to qualify what He meant by *Father, heaven, hallowed, name,* or *kingdom.* He simply used the tried and true metaphors of the Old Testament for speaking to God. Prayer takes in the fullness of life from the coming kingdom to our daily bread and challenges us to participate with God in His work. To ask God for our forgiveness is to enter into the work of forgiveness. To pray for God's kingdom to come is to pray for deliverance from evil. To pray for God's will to be done on earth as it is in heaven is to pray that we obey His Word.

There is no question that in the book of Acts prayer is at the center of the action. Every decision, miracle, event, and advance of the gospel is preceded by prayer, from Pentecost to Paul's witness in Rome. The early church responded to the apostles' teaching through prayer and moved forward in mission by prayer. There can be no doubt that Paul was convinced that the way to hear God's Word was through prayer. He was constantly praying that the Lord would open believers' minds and hearts to the wisdom and revelation of God. No effort was made on Paul's part to elaborate on a prayer ritual or to prescribe a certain formula for prayer. His prayers were personal, passionate, and practical, as illustrated in his prayer for the Ephesians. "I pray that out of his glorious riches he may strengthen you with power through his Spirit in your inner being, so that Christ may dwell in your hearts through faith" (Ephesians 3:16).

For the believer, life's actions are meant to turn on the dialogue between ourselves and the Lord. Real prayer is our response to God's initiative; it is our dialogue with His revelation. The Word on prayer causes us to focus on the Word, rather than on our list-making, repetitive, time-conscious prayers. There is far too much gossip in and around our prayers and far too little gospel in our prayers. *We tend to use prayer to tell our story, when prayer should help us understand how God's story bears on our story.*

Many have been attracted to formulas, such as the popular prayer of Jabez, as a way of hearing the Word prayerfully. Jabez was a man referred to in the book of Chronicles who honored God. He prayed, "Oh, that you would bless me and enlarge my territory! Let your hand be with me, and keep me from harm so that I will be free from pain" (1 Chronicles 4:10); ("that You would keep me from evil, that I may not cause pain!" NKJV; or, "that thou wouldst keep me from harm so that it might not hurt me!" RSV). This is a good prayer, and Jabez was blessed by God for praying it, but the problem comes when we turn this prayer into a slogan for blessing, a proven formula for success.

Believers are encouraged to pray Jabez' prayer for success and safety every day for the rest of their lives. Instead of learning to pray for understanding of God's Word and obedience to Christ in the face of suffering, people are encouraged to look for a miracle for themselves and expect great things.

It is in the Psalms that we learn the scope and depth of real prayer.

It is easy for us to take the prayer of Jabez and lift it out of the biblical text and interpret it according to our self-focused, success-driven, materialistic culture. Never mind that the original disciples were persecuted to death; what seems to matter is God proving Himself in ever-increasing investment portfolios and greater profits. The early disciples seemed far more concerned about proclaiming the greatness of God than feeling the touch of greatness. Instead of extracting a slogan from the Word as a motto for life, they prayed through the whole counsel of God's Word in order to obey it for life.

It seems to me that the prayer of Jabez deserves to be eclipsed by Brother Lawrence's devotional classic, *The Practice of the Presence of God*. It was said of this seventeenth-century monk that there was no difference between the appointed times of prayer and the rest of his day, "because he still continued with God, praising and blessing him with all his might, so that he passed his life in continual joy."[5]

PRAYING THE WORD

Before we hear the Word prayerfully we need to learn to pray according to the Word. The Psalms are our invitation. They call out, "Let us pray." They presuppose that we need instruction in prayer. Prayer has not been left up to our whim and fancy, to our private emotions and haphazard feelings, but to the Spirit's tutoring through the Psalms. We are liberated from the pressure of relying on our own initiative. The Psalms take up the challenge of our feeble use of language and mediocre grasp of reality. They shake up our dull spirits and lethargic spirituality. It is in the Psalms that we learn the scope and depth of real prayer. The Bible's prayer book moves us well beyond our narrow range of emotions, helping us to discover the depths of our soul. "To you, O LORD, I lift up my soul; in you I trust, O my God. Do not let me be put to shame, nor let my enemies triumph over me" (Psalm 25:1–2).

Through the Psalms we are led out of the small world of our making into the large world of God's creation. "When I consider your heavens, the work of your fingers, the moon and the stars, which you have set in place, what is man that you are mindful of him, the son of man that you care for him?" (8:3–4). The Psalms cause us to confront our personal sin, and they teach us how to deal with sin and suffering. We cry out with the psalmist, "Have mercy on me, O God, according to your unfailing love; according to your great compassion blot out my transgressions" (51:1). They guide us in the experience of salvation. "Praise the LORD, O my soul, and forget not all his benefits—who forgives all [my] sins and heals all [my] diseases, who redeems [my] life from the pit and crowns [me] with love and compassion" (103:2–4).

The Psalms help us to go from talking about God to talking to God. Left to ourselves we don't know where to begin. We feel like the disciples: "Lord, teach us to pray" (Luke 11:1). But it is easy to make prayer out to be much harder than it is, or to reduce it to something it was never intended to be. People are tempted to look for an icon or rosary or simple formula to inspire their prayer. They would like to chant or genuflect, but the Psalms resist anything mechanical or formulaic. There is no shortcut to a meaningful relationship to God, nor is there an elaborate ritual that must be followed. The personal intensity and earthy spirituality of the Psalms leads us into an honest relationship with the Lord.

Consider how Psalm 28 helps us to pray the Word. David prays without a hint of posturing. Spurning empty rhetoric, he speaks directly to the Lord. "To you I call, O LORD my Rock; do not turn a deaf ear to me" (Psalm 28:1). There is a note of desperation in this prayer, a sense of passionate intensity right from the start. This is not chitchat conversation, but necessary communication. This way of speaking is deeply rooted in the soul and is by no means a cut-flower prayer. Life is on the line, hanging by a thread, on the edge. The psalmist feels threatened. "For if you remain silent, I will be like those who have gone down to the pit" (v. 1). It's as if David felt he was standing on a precipice overlooking the abyss.

Our natural tendency is to ignore sin and sweep it under the rug.

I remember praying prayers of desperation when my father was dying from cancer. After weeks of heartrending prayers, I felt as though I was all prayed out. I had nothing more to say, but I continued to pray, mindful of the apostle Paul's promise that the Spirit helps us in our weakness. He was right: "We do not know what we ought to pray for, but the Spirit himself intercedes for us with groans that words cannot express" (Romans 8:26).

Not all prayer begins as a desperate cry for help, but many more prayers should begin this way than do! Sadly, we are often oblivious to the trials and dangers we face. We naively go about our business unaware of the dangers around us. It usually takes cancer or a heart attack to get our attention.

But there are many other, more subtle dangers that put us closer to the precipice than we realize. We are surrounded by unhealthy relationships, tempting excesses, and moral shortcuts. David's eyes are wide open to the dangers of the soul. "Hear my cry for mercy as I call to you for help, as I lift up my hands toward your Most Holy Place" (Psalm 28:2). With his whole being he cries out for God. He literally reaches out for God by lifting up his hands; even his body language cries out for God. His words are simple, but well chosen. By addressing the Lord as "my Rock" and referring to His "Most Holy Place," he affirms the security and stability of God. God's strength is not precarious, but his is. There is nothing shaky about God, but the psalmist fears he might fall. He clings to the Rock and reaches for the Most Holy Place.

As in so many psalms, this psalm causes us to confront the pervasiveness of sin and the ever-present threat of evil. Our natural tendency is to ignore sin and sweep it under the rug. We minimize its dangers and assume we can deal with sin by acting as if it weren't there. But in Psalm 28 David has a fresh awareness of the immediacy of evil and a renewed appreciation for his own vulnerability. "Do not drag me away with the wicked, with those who do evil" (v. 3). He doesn't want to be identified with the wicked, particularly with the clever deceivers "who speak cordially with their neighbors but harbor malice in their hearts" (v. 3). He affirms the importance of judgment.

We go beyond curiosity, analysis, and debate and let the Word, by the Holy Spirit, teach, rebuke, correct, and train us in righteousness.

"Repay them for their deeds and for their evil work; repay them for what their hands have done and bring back upon them what they deserve" (v. 4).

On the surface the wicked may get away with positive public relations, but the fact remains, "they show no regard for the works of the LORD and what his hands have done." Consequently, the Lord "will tear them down and never build them up again" (v. 5). What appears as vindictive to the secular mind is the true response of a healthy conscience. David is convinced of the moral necessity of God's judgment.[6] He does not want to be associated with the wicked, nor be dragged down by their deceptive ways. Through prayer he distances himself from their evil ways and affirms his trust in God's justice.

Far from feeling that this psalm is irrelevant or that the psalmist's supplication doesn't relate to us, we are reminded of our own vulnerability. We are led to ask whether we have grown so accustomed to those who "show no regard for the works of the Lord" that we no longer feel the threat of evil. To pray with David is to be pulled out of our sinful indifference and passivity, and led into a longing for God's justice and a dependency upon God's mercy.

David is confident that God has heard his cry. The heaviness of his concern lifts. His passionate intensity shifts from lament to praise. Through prayer he comes to a deeper sense of assurance. "Praise be to the LORD, for he has heard my cry for mercy. The LORD is my strength and my shield; my heart trusts in him, and I am helped. My heart leaps for joy and I will give thanks to him in song" (vv. 6–7). So instead of falling into the pit, he leaps for joy; instead of feeling threatened, he experiences the Lord's protection. Prayer reminds him that the Lord is his strength and shield, and not only for him personally, but for all God's people. "The LORD is the strength of his people, a fortress of salvation for his anointed one" (v. 8).

As the anointed one, King David was conscious that he didn't stand alone. He stood for the people, and the grace that belonged to him was meant for all the people of God. Today we cannot pray this psalm without thinking of Jesus, the Christ, the Anointed One in whom "we have redemption through his blood, the forgiveness of sins, in accordance with the riches of God's grace that he lavished on us with all wisdom and understanding" (Ephesians 1:7–8). David's prayer has been answered beyond anything he imagined, but that does not lessen the significance of this psalm; it only points to its fulfillment.

HEARING THE WORD PRAYERFULLY

Prayer transforms an otherwise routine Bible reading into a personal hearing of the voice of God. When we pray the truth of God's Word, we apply it to our lives. We do not sit in judgment on the Word, deciding what we like or dislike about the Bible's message. Through prayer we embrace the Word. We go beyond curiosity, analysis, and debate and let the Word, by the Holy Spirit, teach, rebuke, correct, and train us in righteousness (2 Timothy 3:16).

We cannot pray the Word without asking if we carry out in practice what we pray for. Charles Spurgeon, the great nineteenth-century British preacher, brought the message of Psalm 28 home in an especially powerful way. He said, "To pray to God for that which I am not willing to promote by my own personal activity is to mock God. . . . O dear friends, let us take care that our prayers do not become swift witnesses against us to condemn us."[7] To pray as David did in Psalm 28, "Save your people," is "to put myself constantly on the alert to be the instrument of saving God's people."[8] To ask God to bless His inheritance is to bless that inheritance ourselves. Spurgeon admonished, "Take care that *you* bless them. So far as is in your power, seek to confer blessings upon all your fellow Christians."[9] How can we ask the Lord to be their shepherd and then act like wolves ready to bite and devour them (Galatians 5:15)? To pray the Word is to live the Word.

Andy and Rebecca DesRoches, missionaries

in Beira, Mozambique, illustrate what it means to pray the Word. In a recent letter they began with Psalm 16:2, "I said to the LORD, 'You are my Lord; apart from you I have no good thing." They used this psalm to recall the many good things the Lord had given them, such as "good and fulfilling work, good people to work with, good health, and a good missionary community." They affirmed that "apart from the Lord Jesus" they would have none of these good things and would not be able to serve Him in Mozambique.

They prayed Psalm 37, "Trust in the LORD and do good; dwell in the land and enjoy safe pasture. Delight yourself in the LORD and he will give you the desires of your heart" (vv. 3–4). They recounted how the Lord has given them the desires of their hearts by sending them to a people who want to learn and grow in their faith, by giving them the privilege of ministering to the poor and bringing hope, and by allowing them to use their gifts in special ways.

One of their big concerns was how life in Mozambique would affect their children, Samuel and Davita. But after fifteen months they could say, "The Lord is working in the lives of our children, shaping them and bringing them to maturity." Through prayer, Andy and Rebecca hear the Word of God and apply it to their lives. Their letter closed with Psalm 16:8, "I have set the LORD always before me. Because he is at my right hand, I will not be shaken." Through prayer, they are learning to use God's Word as a light for their path (Psalm 119:105).

4
MODEL
THE WORD

Be perfect, therefore, as your heavenly Father is perfect.
MATTHEW 5:48

*B*iblical revelation comes to us in a variety of ways. Like a prism refracting light into a rainbow of colors, God's Word splits the light of truth into a multimedia presentation of clear prose, true stories, passionate poetry, powerful visions, defining precepts, and engaging parables. Some people want us to believe that God's message is subject to their careful background checks and scholarly approval. Others contend that they hold the secret key to unlock the interpretative mystery. But for those who are willing to listen to the Word of God on its own terms, the Message is powerful and penetrating.

Our job is not to interpret the Bible as much as it is to be interpreted by the Bible. As the author of Hebrews wrote, "The word of God is living and active. Sharper than any double-edged sword, it penetrates even to dividing soul and spirit, joints and marrow; it judges the thoughts and attitudes of the heart" (Hebrews 4:12). Much is hidden from our eyes, but "nothing in all creation is hidden from God's sight" (v. 13); therefore it makes sense to listen to God's Word with open ears and an open mind.

Parables are the Bible's version of going to the movies.

One of the great ways the Word of God gets us to pay attention to the truth is through parables. Parables are simple, vivid stories, often drawn from ordinary life, which illustrate truth in profound and meaningful ways. Parables may either unsettle or inspire, but they do not lecture. They draw us into the drama of God's will and invite us to respond. Parables avoid reducing life to list making. They do not confuse truth with technique. Parables are the Bible's version of going to the movies. They help us to visualize the impact of God's truth in our real life situation. As role-playing models, parables are a significant element in God's instructional strategy. They help us see ourselves and evaluate our own reaction to God's message.

At first glance, the Bible doesn't seem to have much to say about parenting, especially if we are looking for a how-to section. There appears to be a real lack of explicit prescriptive material on parenting in the Bible. We don't find a list of the ten easy steps for effective parenting in the Bible, but what we do find is God's wisdom in how to hold our children in our hearts. Instead of being given a set of parenting dos and don'ts, we learn what it means to be like our heavenly Father. We discover the relationship between being in Christ and becoming a good parent.

Our job is not to interpret the Bible as much as it is to be interpreted by the Bible.

A PARABLE ON PARENTING

The Parable of the Lost Son is a good example of how the Bible teaches us to be good parents.

In a strict sense, the parable has nothing to do with parenting skills and how to be a father. It is about God's persistent, passionate grace for the lost. It is in the context of the parables of the lost sheep and the lost coin. God goes out of His way to find that which is lost. The Lord is like the shepherd who leaves his flock in the open country and goes after the lost sheep until he finds it. The Lord is like the woman who will not rest until she finds her lost coin. The audience for these three parables is divided into two groups. There are "tax collectors and 'sinners'" who have gathered around Jesus "to hear him," and there are Pharisees and the teachers of the law who stand on the edge of the crowd muttering among themselves, "This man welcomes sinners and eats with them" (Luke 15:1–2). Luke encourages us to see the difference: Are we ready to listen or are we here to mutter?

All three parables focus on God's grace extended to the lost for the sake of their salvation. The first two set up the third more involved story, the parable of the lost son. The purpose of the parables reminds us of the purpose of parenting. For parents who follow Jesus, the core issue is not educating their children for a successful career.

It is not about raising them so that they are decent, law-abiding, drug-free, nice people. It is about parenting in such a way that our daughters and sons respond to the grace of God offered to lost sinners for the sake of their salvation. It is about our children receiving the heavenly Father's love and grace, and responding to that love. In a life-changing way, this parable offers a powerful model in how to be a parent like our heavenly Father. Parents, particularly fathers, cannot hear this parable without comparing themselves to the father in the parable.

The parable invites us to put ourselves in the shoes of all three characters. If we are in the "far country," alienated and estranged from God, we are invited to come home and experience the love of God. If we are like the older son, dutiful, religious, merit conscious, but unaware of God's grace and mercy, we are invited to celebrate the Father's love and enter into the joy of the Lord. However, we often miss the invitation to model ourselves after the main character in the parable, the loving Father. We are hesitant about contemplating the father as a model for our love, even though it is natural for a parent reading this story to put himself in the place of the father.

Our reserve may be due to the fact that we identify the father's love in the parable with our heavenly Father's love for the world, and we question the appropriateness of trying to imitate God's love. This reluctance, however, may have more to do with avoiding our responsibility than showing reverence for God. To see the heavenly Father's love as the model

Your heavenly Father stands ready to embrace you.

for our love sets the bar far too high for those who think humanistically; but for those who hear the Word, it is the goal for which they seek. Didn't Jesus dismiss this false deference when He said in the Sermon on the Mount, "Be perfect, therefore, as your heavenly Father is perfect" (Matthew 5:48)? He expected the righteousness of His followers to surpass the righteousness of the Pharisees and the teachers of the law (v. 20), not in any kind of sinless perfection, but in a grown-up attitude reflecting their God-created identity.

It is fitting for a true child of God to take after the heavenly Father. Instead of reacting against others with resentment, revenge, and retaliation,

Jesus called for an alternative model based on the Father's love. Our family likeness comes through "when we love with an all-embracing love like his."[1] As Jesus said, "whoever does the will of my Father in heaven is my brother and sister and mother" (Matthew 12:50). The power of this parable is found not only in receiving the heavenly Father's embrace but in modeling the heavenly Father's love in our families.

PRODIGAL FATHERS

Lost sons who don't come to their senses become prodigal fathers. There is no age limit on running away from God or resenting the Father's love. Fathers can easily reach their forties or fifties and still refuse to come home. They can starve to death emotionally and spiritually in the far country, having cut themselves off from their Lord and their family. Recently a friend of mine buried his father, whom he had not seen for years. His father abandoned the family twenty-eight years ago when he ran off with another woman. He moved around the country, seldom spending more than a year in one place, until he died in a trailer park in Florida. If it had not been for the persistence of some of his father's friends in the trailer park, my friend might never have learned of his father's death.

Some people cannot read the parable of the prodigal son without feeling the pain and loss of having a prodigal father. The Father pictured in the parable is far removed from the father they have experienced in life. Surely one of our basic and strongest impulses is to be related to our parents in the bond of love, and when that relationship is frustrated by abandonment, abuse, disinterest, or selfishness, we are in pain. Oftentimes this pain impacts our relationship to our heavenly Father. Some people feel they cannot experience, let alone imagine, God's love, because of the brokenness in their families. They feel as if they are living in the far country, destitute of love and support, due to no fault of their own.

For all those who identify with the pain and brokenness of the lost son in the far country, but who feel there is no place to come home to, remember that this parable is about the heavenly Father's love for the lost. In spite of prodigal fathers, God's love is there to redeem, forgive, restore, and reconcile you to Himself. Like the father in the story, your heavenly Father stands ready to embrace you. The parable affirms the psalmist's hope: "Though my father and mother forsake me, the LORD will receive me" (Psalm 27:10).

TYPICAL FATHERS

The father pictured in the parable is not a typical father in any culture, either ancient or modern. When Jesus told this story, He fought the stereotype. In our culture, "we are told that a real man provides for the family and leaves the emotional stuff for the woman in the house," but that is not the picture we get in this parable.[2] You may have read the amusing "Real Man" quiz that was on the Internet. It went something like this:

You're awakened by your wife early in the morning. She tells you that she is sick and that you will have to get the three children ready for school today. Your response is:
    a. Do they need to eat or anything?
    b. They're in school already?
    c. There are three of them?

This may be funny because it reminds us of the common stereotype that says men don't get involved in parenting, but it is truly sad when fathers are emotionally distant from their daughters and sons. If we want a healthy relationship with our children, "we need to learn the language of feelings that may not come naturally to us."[3] We need to spend quality and quantity time with our children. As professor Mark McMinn encourages, "We can share the tenderhearted privilege of parenting with our wives if we break through the unfortunate stereotypes of being male."[4]

In Jesus' parable there is no hint of a father out of touch with his children or emotionally distant. The father pictured here is fully present, emotionally engaged, and responsive to both sons. He is neither passive nor aggressive but sensitive to his sons, and he is very capable of using the language of love.

Biblical scholars have made much of the fact that the father pictured in Jesus' parable does not fit the Middle Eastern stereotype of a father. What father would divide up his property and give his son a share of his inheritance before he died? The younger son's request is tantamount to wishing that the father had died. What self-respecting Middle Eastern father would humiliate himself by running to his estranged son, throw his arms

around him, and kiss him? Scholars find it difficult to imagine a father pleading with the older
son to accept his decision to kill the fattened calf.
Not only does the father suffer the shame of a rebellious son but then shames himself by lower-
ing himself in the eyes of the culture. First, he
gives up his inheritance, then he lavishes affec-
tion on his wayward son when he returns home,
and finally, he pleads with his hard-hearted older
son. The father in the parable is highly unusual. He
appears to have little concern for Middle Eastern
dignity and reserve, and he lets his affections
transcend his authority. Love for his sons su-
percedes all cultural expectations of what a father should be like.

What scholars do not seem to realize is that
Jesus' description of the father is not colored by
culture but by biblical revelation. Jesus has in
mind the heavenly Father, not your typical Middle Eastern father. It may be dramatically incon-
sistent for a Middle Eastern father to divide up
the inheritance before he dies, but God the Father does it all the time. "He causes his sun to rise
on the evil and the good, and sends rain on the
righteous and the unrighteous" (Matthew 5:45).
God blesses rebellious prodigals with good health

and great talents all the time. A Middle Eastern father may find it humiliating to run after his son and display such compassion, but our heavenly Father is known for His love.

> As a father has compassion on his children,
>   so the LORD has compassion on
>   those who fear him;
> for he knows how we are formed,
>   he remembers that we are dust.
>
> (Psalm 103:13–14)

Like God the Father, the father in the parable is not willing that any should be lost (Matthew 18:14), but that "everyone . . . come to repentance" (2 Peter 3:9). A Middle Eastern father might have disowned his son and cut him off, but not the Father in the mind of Jesus, who is known as the "Wonderful Counselor, Mighty God, Everlasting Father, Prince of Peace" (Isaiah 9:6). A Middle Eastern father might have never pleaded with his older son, but our heavenly Father is entreating us all the time. From the perspective of Jesus, the father in the parable of the lost son is meant to remind us of our heavenly Father. He is worthy of the apostle Paul's commendation,

"Praise be to the God and Father of our Lord Jesus Christ, the Father of compassion and the God of all comfort" (2 Corinthians 1:3).

THE LOVING FATHER

Parents who are concerned about their children coming to God can learn a great deal from how Jesus shows us the heavenly Father's love. This parable encourages us to put ourselves in the place of the father and model our love for our children after God's gracious love for us.

First, it strikes me as ironic that a parable that pictures the heavenly Father's love should tell the story of a rebellious son and a resentful son. Clearly the failure of the sons is no reflection on the father. They do not fail because of some deficiency or inadequacy on the part of the father, but because of their own willful reaction against the father. Unlike our heavenly Father,

Grace is the outstanding characteristic of the father's response to his prodigal son.

we make mistakes. No parent is perfect and many of us have a keen sense of our inadequacy, but good parents can have rebellious, resentful children. Sometimes we stop showing the love we should because we feel like failures. We let the spiritual passivity or spiritual resistance of our children get to us. We blame ourselves for their rebellion, and we cultivate deep feelings of failure. The father in the parable is able to continue loving his sons because he does not absorb their failure as his own. We should learn from this model. Blaming ourselves for sons or daughters who insist on going into the far country and living as they please will interfere with loving them and praying for them.

Second, it is significant that the rebellious son had to leave his father's presence to live as he pleased. As long as he lived at home, he was not free to engage in wild living. Grace is the outstanding characteristic of the father's response to his prodigal son, but such grace is evident only against the background of law. If the father had been a permissive father instead of a loving father the son could have done just as he pleased in the presence of the father. The fact that he could not points to the controlling, unyielding, God-honoring will of the father. In fact, the law of the father undoubtedly contributed to the younger son's radical and rebellious request for his inheritance. The father's love placed limits on the freedom of the younger son, who found it necessary to distance himself from the presence of the father.

In the parable, there is a profound sense of the distance between the presence of the father and the far country, but this is often not the case today. Prodigal sons and daughters do as they please and still live at home. Christian parents often tolerate children who show little respect for parental authority or obedience to the clearly revealed will of God. I believe the parable is instructive at this point. A Christian way of life and a pagan way of life cannot co-exist in the same household, at least not for an extended period of time. Prodigals should move out, even if it means that they receive a portion of their inheritance!

The grace of God is not grasped until we see our own wickedness.

On the other hand, the Christian community has gone along in naively instituting a rite of passage for prodigals by sending them off to college. The university has become the occasion for many young people raised in Christian homes to squander wealth and, more importantly, their lives, in wild living without being defined as prodigals. There is no clear break with what their Christian home stands for, but their rejection of God's will is evident in their lives and they become victims of their choices just as the prodigal son.

Even as God's love for us is immediate, costly, and unreserved, so should ours be.

What is important for us to see is that the grace and compassion of the father for his son is completely consistent with the son's inability to live any way he pleased in the presence of his father. Law and grace always go together in the will of God.

Third, the son's experience in the far country confirms what we know of the world. The world affords the freedom to live as we please, but it is capable of great cruelty. For a while, a selfish world may be a fun and exciting place to be, but inevitably a selfish world turns against you and makes you one of its victims, whether through addiction or success, poverty or luxury, loneliness or fame. The pursuit of selfishness always proves terminal. When the prodigal "came to his senses" (Luke 15:17), he couldn't stop thinking about his father. He knew he didn't merit the father's love, but he needed the father's love. "So he got up and went to his father" (v. 20). The goodness of God is often not perceived until we see the evil of the world. The grace of God is not grasped until we see our own wickedness.

Fourth, we can learn from the unconditional love of our heavenly Father how to love our children. If our children have rejected the grace of God, we can love them by longing for their return and being prepared to welcome them with open arms. Love is demonstrated not only in the embrace that comes at the end of the journey home, but in the waiting and praying that parents do as they hold their children in their heart. Parents who have experienced the embrace of the Father for themselves ought to see themselves in the love of the waiting father. We are not only the recipients of this love but also the communicators of this love. The description of the father's love helps us to visualize what our love should be like. "But while he was still a long way off, his father saw him and was filled with compassion for him; he ran to his son, threw his arms around him and kissed him" (v. 20). Even as God's love for us is immediate, costly, and unreserved, so should ours be. Love holds nothing back. "Quick! Bring the best robe and put it on him. Put a ring on his finger and sandals on his feet. Bring the fattened calf and kill it. Let's have a feast and celebrate. For this son of mine was dead and is alive again; he was lost and is found" (vv. 22–24).

Fifth, not only do prodigal sons sometimes become prodigal fathers, but resentful sons can become resentful fathers. They may be decent, hardworking fathers, but they measure life by what they achieve, not by the grace they receive. They resist becoming loving fathers. In the parable, the oldest son lives in the presence of his father's love without ever paying attention to his father's heart or entering into his father's passion. He has all the privileges of sonship but feels like a hired hand, bound by duty, slaving away. Is the father to blame for his oldest son's resentment? The son accuses his father of favoritism and ingratitude. "You never gave me even a young goat so I could celebrate with my friends" (v. 29). But the charges are groundless. Far from being indifferent, the loving father has left the celebration to plead with his oldest son. The resentful son refers to his brother as "this son of yours" (v. 30) and insists on defining him by his sinful past, but the loving father pleads with his oldest son, "My son, you are always with me, and everything I have is yours. But we had to celebrate and be glad, because this brother of yours was dead and is alive again; he was lost and is found" (vv. 31–32). The oldest son could write off his younger brother with a derogatory reference to *"this son of yours,"* but the loving father insists on celebrating, "because *this brother of yours* . . . was lost and is found."

In the parable of the prodigal son, it is the example of the father's love that catches the attention of fathers. If our heavenly Father "did not spare his own Son, but gave him up for us all" (Romans 8:32), how then shall we love our daughters and sons? If our heavenly Father has embraced us by His grace through the forgiveness of our sin, how much more should we be willing to love our children and do whatever it takes to show them the love of God in Christ?

5

PICTURE THE WORD

Do you want to be counted wise, to build a reputation for wisdom? Here's what you do: Live well, live wisely, live humbly. It's the way you live, not the way you talk, that counts.

JAMES 3:13 THE MESSAGE

There is a close relationship between hearing the Word of God and seeing God's wisdom portrayed. Vivid biblical word pictures help us visualize the truth of God. Proverbs 31 is a classic example of truth *pictured* rather than lectured. Wisdom is described in real-world earth tones rather than defined in idealistic platitudes. To hear the Word of God in Proverbs 31 is to let the portrait of a wise woman shape and color our perspective on wisdom. It is not a still life portrait, but a series of action pictures that captures both the essence and the multifaceted nature of wisdom. Instead of being given a list of ideas, we are invited to picture a life of faithfulness, fellowship, and fidelity. Like a beautiful painting, it deserves our careful attention and our appreciation for the artist's medium and cultural period.

Anyone can judge a painting according to his or her biases and prejudices, but it often takes careful work to discover and appreciate the real beauty of a work of art. The woman pictured in Proverbs 31 lives well, lives wisely, lives humbly. Her portrait was meant to inspire wisdom, not envy, and help both women and men picture what the "fear of the LORD" (v. 30) looks like in daily life.

A friend observed that pastors use Father's Day to admonish men how to be better fathers, but on Mother's Day the church praises mothers for how great they are! At first glance this biblical passage would appear to reverse this pattern. For many, the picture illustrated in Proverbs 31 may be more intimidating than inspiring. It impresses some as an ode to Super Mom. It projects an idealistic image of a woman who has it all together. Instead of encouraging women, this picture may have a reverse effect—it may discourage mothers and make them feel inferior. Who can compete with this kind of woman? I'm sure a few people read Proverbs 31 and picture Martha Stewart, the high priestess of perfectionism.

Recently a friend was in the checkout line at the grocery with his wife. He was glancing at the magazines when his eye caught the cover of *Vogue*. He focused for a moment on the bikini clad model before intentionally averting his eyes. His wife, who had observed his reaction, walked over to the magazine rack, picked up a copy of *Vogue*, pointed to the model, and said, "I can't compete with that!"

This can be an especially hard and competitive culture for women. It is both ironic and embarrassing that our culture tends to measure a woman's worth by her measurements. We have fixated on weight rather than worth, and sex appeal rather than character. The less a woman weighs the greater her value, and the more she attends to her physical appearance the more attention she receives. I know a person who recently turned

Wisdom is devotion to the truth and the discernment of right and wrong.

down a job in a wealthy suburb of Dallas. One of the considerations that he and his wife discussed was the culture of intimidation generated by women who spend lavishly on clothes and cosmetics and worry incessantly about their weight. Having lived in an up-scale culture before, his wife was reluctant to reenter the image wars and battle feelings of inferiority.

There are several key insights which help in understanding this important picture of wisdom in Proverbs. The real impact of this picture is not to indict, but to encourage. Instead of making women feel inferior, the conclusion of Proverbs empowers women. But in order for this picture of wisdom to have its true impact, it is helpful to discern several significant differences: (1) the difference between the fear of the Lord and the fear of what other people think of us; (2) the difference between biblical perfection and cultural perfection; and (3) the difference between true heartfelt praise and halfhearted appreciation.

TWO TYPES OF FEAR

Of all the ways the book of Proverbs might have ended, it is significant that it ends with a life picture of a woman. The theme of the book is all about wisdom—real world, down-to-earth, everyday wisdom. Chapter one begins with a word picture. The "plain daylight of wisdom" is refracted "into its rainbow of constituent colors."[1] Wisdom is devotion to the truth and the discernment of right and wrong. It is discretion, discipline, and diligence. Wisdom involves giving and receiving direction and guidance. It's not about being smart or brilliant or having a high I.Q. It's about having insight and understanding. It's about learning to listen and listening to learn. The starting point and bottom line for this full-orbed, multifaceted, personally engaging wisdom is this: "The fear of the LORD is the beginning of knowledge, but fools despise wisdom and discipline" (Proverbs 1:7).

As Proverbs continues, wisdom is applied in every conceivable area of life from speech to sex; from sloth to success. There is virtually nothing in life that doesn't call for wisdom. It ranges from common sense to Creation's core value. When wisdom is personified in Proverbs, the feminine voice is used. Wisdom raises *her* voice, and *she* cries out at the city gates (Proverbs 8:1–11). In a description that makes us think of Christ Himself, "in whom are hidden all the treasures of wisdom and knowledge" (Colossians 2:3), we are told that wisdom was from the beginning (vv. 22–31).

All that is said about wisdom, from the word picture to the Christ picture, only makes the life picture at the end all the more significant. We might have anticipated some sage advice or a special description of the king as a fitting model for wisdom, but instead, we see a woman whose whole life is compellingly shaped by the fear of the Lord. This portrait is not a fragment attached to the end simply because it doesn't fit anywhere else. On the contrary, it is the writer's climax. It is the closing illustration that brings the message home. By the time you get to the end of Proverbs we're asking, "What does wisdom look like?" And the writer shows us. I can't imagine a stronger way of honoring women than using a woman to capture the essence of wisdom and the fear of the Lord. The conclusion of Proverbs is a resounding affirmation of the significance of the *wisdom* of women who honor God.

The confidence and competence that this woman exudes is derived from her fear of the Lord. Her sense of awe and her reverence for God overcome her fears of inferiority, intimidation, self-doubt, and timidity. By fearing the Lord, she is not fearful of her husband or frustrated by changing circumstances or frightened by the future. Through dependence and devotion to God, she gains an essential perspective for dealing with life. The fear of the Lord opposes the fear of what others think of us. It shrinks the fears that confine us to the small world of other people's

Cultural perfectionism triggers envy, but biblical perfection inspires growth.

expectations. As we respond to God in reverence and awe, we react less and less to the pressures that intimidate and belittle us.

The fear of the Lord has enlarged this woman's world. She is free to enjoy and contribute to her husband and her children. She shows compassion to the poor and cares for those who work under her authority. She is creative, energetic, and wise. She and her husband work as a team. She manages the household, invests in real estate, and plans ahead. The fear of the Lord has liberated this woman in ways the modern woman envies. Her life is full and her world is whole because her character is rooted in the wisdom of God.

TWO FORMS OF PERFECTION

Women who are intimidated by this picture of wisdom may find it helpful to distinguish between cultural and biblical perfection. The woman described in Proverbs 31 as a woman of noble character who fears the Lord and is clothed with strength and dignity would laugh at the comparison between herself and Martha Stewart. The writer Kathleen Norris observes that perfectionism is "a serious psychological affliction that makes people too timid to take necessary risks and causes them to suffer when, although they've done the best they can, their efforts fall short of some imaginary, and usually unattainable, standard." She calls Martha Stewart "the high priestess of Perfection: one dare not let the mask slip, even in one's home, where all is perfect, right down to the last hand-stenciled napkin ring."[2] Perfectionism is not a compliment, but a disorder. It describes those who have reduced life to a compulsive self-preoccupied performance. Perfectionism flattens life out and makes flower arrangements as important as feeding the hungry.

This is not the perfection that Jesus had in mind in the Sermon on the Mount when he admonished, "Be perfect . . . as your heavenly Father is perfect" (Matthew 5:48). Nor is it true to the apostle Paul's understanding when he wrote, "We proclaim him, admonishing and teaching everyone with all wisdom, so that we may present everyone perfect in Christ" (Colossians 1:28). The biblical understanding of perfection involves growth and maturity. It has to do with holiness and righteousness. As Kathleen Norris writes, "To 'be perfect,' in the sense that Jesus means it, is to make room for growth, for the changes that bring us to maturity, to ripeness. To mature is to lose adolescent self-consciousness so as to be able to make a gift of oneself, as a parent, as teacher, friend, spouse."[3]

The difference between cultural and biblical perfection is the difference between cosmetics and character, etiquette and ethics, interior decorating and heartfelt devotion. It is the difference between cut flowers and the tree of righteousness. One form of perfection is preoccupied with the latest fashions and the other is concerned with enduring faithfulness. That is not to say that the woman in Proverbs 31 is all substance and no style. There is ample evidence that this woman knows how to dress with style and has an eye for beauty, but appearances do not rule her life. She is a woman of character and maturity who seeks first things first.

Cultural perfectionism triggers envy, but biblical perfection inspires growth. There is a difference between envying someone and aspiring to be like them. If we take a careful look at the woman of noble character, without the ghost of Martha Stewart looming in the background, we see a woman who we would like to have as a friend or a mentor. Her example raises us up rather than puts us down. We are encouraged by her, rather than intimidated by her. If people of maturity and character provoke resentment and anger within us, the problem lies not with them, but within us. I suppose someone reading Proverbs 31 could envy this woman for her happy marriage, respectful children, profitable business, and energetic creativity, or they could learn from her. Such a choice lies with us and distinguishes wisdom from foolishness.

TWO KINDS OF RECOGNITION

Some people spend considerable energy trying to win the favor of people in general, rather than the people they know. Fame is name recognition by the nameless masses, but family is knowing that you are loved by those closest to you. For some people, it is far more important to be popular than to be loved. They confuse these two and see popularity as a substitute for intimacy. Some women and some men long for public recognition because of their broken personal relationships. They compete for people's approval, because they are not secure in their family's love. They have not learned the difference between fearing God and fearing what other people think; they have not distinguished between biblical perfection and cultural perfection; nor have they understood that cultivating noble character is not the same as doing noble things.

There is a huge difference between heartfelt praise and halfhearted appreciation. Obviously, the difference cannot be measured in flowery words or expensive gifts. I love the way this woman is praised and honored. "Her children arise and call her blessed" (Proverbs 31:28). I love it, because I can see it. I can picture the scene. The family is gathered, and a daughter, speaking from her heart and without embarrassment, affirms her mother with the dignity and devotion she deserves. A son stands and speaks up for her because he is proud of her. They acknowledge her wisdom, creativity, energy, and love, not with superlatives, but with a single God-centric word. They call her *blessed.* Her life is an expression of God's work, God's love, God's blessing. She is defined not by what she has achieved, but by what she has received from the hand of God. This affirmation means more than all the flowers and diamonds in the world. Yes! It really does.

Her husband also praises her. He's a discerning man. He values the "right stuff." He draws a comparison that puts his finger right on the key difference: "Many women do noble things, but you surpass them all" (v. 29). The difference is between a woman of noble character who fears the Lord, and a woman who does nice things. There really is no comparison, is there? The measure of a women is not an itemized list of the things she does, but who she is. Here is a woman who ages with grace and becomes more, not less, over time. She has "one foot already in eternity, regarding the time, the

May we value what is truly valuable and praise what is truly praiseworthy.

date, and even the year as being of little consequence."[4]

Her beauty is not skin deep but from the soul, impacting everything she does. She is neither the self-made independent modern woman, nor the small-minded, male-dominated housewife. To praise her is to praise her Lord. Everything she has comes from the Lord, but that in no way distracts from the reward she deserves in and outside the home. "Charm is deceptive, and beauty is fleeting; but a woman who fears the LORD is to be praised. Give her the reward she has earned, and let her works bring her praise at the city gate" (Proverbs 31:30–31).

WISDOM'S COVER GIRL

True wisdom is never abstract and theoretical, as we readily see in this life picture of wisdom's cover girl. You'll never find her on the cover of *Vogue,* but you will find her in the household of faith. Recently a friend was on a subway in New York City when she observed an overweight, sloppily dressed woman reading *Cosmopolitan* magazine. This is the kind of magazine that pictures virtual-reality women whose pictures are carefully composed and computer enhanced. It is debatable whether such women exist in real life. The woman's child was at her side clamoring for attention, but she paid him none. She treated her son with total indifference as she concentrated on the glossy pictures of models portraying a world far beyond her own. My friend's observation was that this mother was escaping her world and sacrificing her son in the process. The real world was at her knee calling for love, but her mind was filled with false images of perfection.

The conclusion of the book of Proverbs opens with a question, "A wife of noble character who can find?" (Proverbs 31:10). The question could be read in various ways. I don't think it means that such a woman is impossible to find. I think it means that when you find such a woman, realize just how priceless she is and accord her the dignity and praise she deserves. As men and women of God may we value what is truly valuable and praise what is truly praiseworthy, so that our children may learn what it means to fear the Lord and grow up in Christ. Is it too much to ask, when our children read the ancient picture of wisdom of Proverbs 31, that they visualize their parents?

6
SING THE WORD

Let the word of Christ dwell in you richly as you teach and admonish one another with all wisdom, and as you sing psalms, hymns and spiritual songs with gratitude in your hearts to God.

COLOSSIANS 3:16

*M*usic is a gift from God that helps us take in the intelligible revelation of God. The prophet Ezekiel was told, "Eat this [book]; then go and speak to the house of Israel." "So I opened my mouth," Ezekiel writes, "and he gave me the [book] to eat" (Ezekiel 3:1–2). Eating the Word of God meant internalizing the truth of God in order to empower the prophet for ministry. In that sense, singing the Word of God "with gratitude in [our] hearts to God" is another picture that helps us grasp what it means to take in the truth of God. To open our mouths and eat the Word has the same meaning as to open our mouths and sing the Word from our hearts. I remember my father's tenor voice singing hymns of the Word more than I recall him speaking about the Word. He never gave a sermon, but he sang from his soul. One of his favorite songs reads,

> All that thrills my soul is Jesus.
> He is more than life to me;
> He, the fairest of ten thousand,
> Is my precious Lord to me.

In his letter to the church at Ephesus, Paul contrasted alcoholic intoxication with being filled with the Spirit. "Do not get drunk on wine, which leads to debauchery. Instead, be filled with the Spirit. Speak to one another with psalms, hymns and spiritual songs" (Ephesians 5:18–19). The evidence of being filled with the Spirit is an outpouring of praise and gratitude. "Sing and make music in your heart to the Lord, always giving thanks to God the Father for everything, in the name of our Lord Jesus Christ" (vv. 19–20). Inter-

Music is inspired by the God who sings.

nalizing the Word of God not only nourishes the soul but it also makes the heart sing.

FAITH SEEKS EXPRESSION

When it came to knowing the Word of God, the apostle Paul found it impossible to separate the mind and heart. Faith in Christ seeks both in-depth understanding and heartfelt expression. Proclamation and praise go hand in hand. Worship is a matter of thinking and feeling. It is both intellectual and emotional, because it engages the mind and expresses the heart. As Henry Mitchell, an African-American pastor, liked to say, "If truth goes into your heart on the arm of emotion it will stay. But if it enters your heart unaccompanied, it will only visit for a short while and then leave." Teaching and singing the Word of God in the household of faith are two actions that belong together. When the church teaches with wisdom and sings with gratitude, our minds and our hearts are informed and inspired by the Word of God.

Throughout the Word of God, music is inspired by the God who sings. Melody, harmony, rhythm, and tone are not human inventions.

David credited his musical ability to God. "He put a new song in my mouth, a hymn of praise to our God" (Psalm 40:3). Israel's priests gave God the credit for the song they sang. "By day the LORD directs his love, at night his song is with me—a prayer to the God of my life" (Psalm 42:8). Music belongs to God the Chief Musician, whose acoustical world resonates with song because God designed not only the voice and ear, but also the heart and spirit. Whatever creativity we express comes from God the Creator who not only inspires the praise but also gives us the gifts with which to express His praise.

The prophet Zephaniah challenged the people of God to sing: "Sing, O Daughter of Zion; shout aloud, O Israel! Be glad and rejoice with all your heart." The reason they could sing was because God rejoiced over them in song. "The LORD your God is with you, he is mighty to save. He will take great delight in you, he will quiet you with his love, he will rejoice over you with singing" (Zephaniah 3:14, 17).

The story of the people of God is not only spoken but sung. The prophet Isaiah described God's love in a love song. "I will sing for the one I love a song about his vineyard" (Isaiah 5:1). Jesus sang with His disciples, such as the time He sang a hymn with them at the Last Supper (Matthew 26:30); and according to the author of Hebrews, He continues to sing, "I will declare your name to my brothers; in the presence of the congregation I will sing your praises"

The Psalms call us into worship.

(Hebrews 2:12). To be filled with the Spirit of God is to "sing and make music" in our heart "to the Lord" (Ephesians 5:19).

From the beginning, music has accompanied the work of God. Creation was formed "while the morning stars sang together and all the angels shouted for joy" (Job 38:7). Surely it is impossible for us to imagine "the heavens [declaring] the glory of God" in a monotone or "the skies [proclaiming] the work of his hands" in a whisper (Psalm 19:1). "The hills are alive with the sound of music" is biblical truth. When Moses and the Israelites crossed the Red Sea, they celebrated the Exodus with a song to the Lord, which began, "I will sing to the LORD, for he is highly exalted." The Lord had done more than give them something to sing about. The Lord Himself was their song. Moses sang, "The LORD is my strength and my song; he has become my salvation. He is my God, and I will praise him, my father's God, and I will exalt him" (Exodus 15:1–2).

Filled with the Spirit, King David led the people of God in song. From lamentation to celebration, David expressed the full range of the Word of God in song. "Your decrees are the theme of my song wherever I lodge" (Psalm 119:54). The Psalms call us into worship with vigorous songs of praise, "Come, let us sing for joy to the LORD; let us shout aloud to the Rock of our salvation. Let us come before him with thanksgiving and extol him with music and song" (95:1–2). Worship is exuberant, "Shout for joy to the LORD, all the earth. Worship the LORD with gladness; come before him with joyful songs" (100:1–2). It is fresh and vital, "Sing to the LORD a new song; sing to the LORD, all the earth.

Worship is not a matter of self-expression but of Word-focused, Christ-centered concentration.

Sing to the LORD, praise his name; proclaim his salvation day after day. Declare his glory among the nations, his marvelous deeds among all peoples" (96:1–3). We have a song to be sung to the nations that will turn their hearts to the Lord.

Music tells God's great salvation history story in song. The dramatic turning points and break-throughs in God's revelation are marked by hymns of praise. Prose gives way to poetry and dialogue to doxology. Narrative becomes declar-ative in anthems of praise. The Exodus is marked by the Song of Moses (Exodus 15). The birth of Christ is celebrated in Mary's Magnificat (Luke 1:46–55), Zechariah's *Benedictus* (vv. 67–79), and the Song of Simeon (2:29–32). Angels offer up an exclamation of praise in the *Gloria* (v. 14). The song of salvation was in the confession and praise of Christ in the early church. His humility and exaltation is celebrated in Paul's letter to the be-lievers at Philippi in what is thought to be an early worship hymn (Philippians 2:6–11). Early Christians confessed in song, "He appeared in a body, was vindicated by the Spirit, was seen by angels, was preached among the nations, was believed on in the world, was taken up in glory" (1 Timothy 3:16).

The book of Revelation anticipates powerful singing in the presence of God:

Hymns of adoration: "Holy, holy, holy is the Lord God Almighty, who was, and is, and is to come" (Revelation 4:8).

Songs of redemption: "You are worthy to take the scroll and to open its seals, because you were slain, and with your blood you purchased [people] for God from every tribe and language and people and nation" (Revelation 5:9).

Anthems of glory, sung with energy and enthusiasm: "Worthy is the Lamb, who was slain, to receive power and wealth and wisdom and strength and honor and glory and praise!" (Revelation 5:12).

The reason the apostle John interchanged "saying" and "singing" in his description of heaven's worship was because he stressed the content of the message that was sung (Revelation 4:8, 10; 5:9, 12; 7:10, 12). No matter how awesome a heavenly choir of "ten thousand times ten thousand" will sound, the message will never be lost in the power of the music (5:11). God's entire salvation history story will be set to music from "the song of Moses the servant of God" to "the song of the Lamb," and all people will worship before the "King of the ages" (15:3).

IN TUNE WITH GOD

As we might expect excellence in worship, music is assumed throughout the Bible. How can we worship God with anything less than our best? In the Old Testament, the ministers of music were priests "trained and skilled in music for the LORD" (1 Chronicles 25:7). Leadership in worship was assigned according to a priest's musical aptitude and skill (15:22). In the New Testament, the priesthood of the believers understood that musical ability is a gift of the Spirit. Hymns come first in Paul's list of gifts that edify the body of believers, ahead of words of instruction and speaking in tongues (1 Corinthians 14:26). Being gifted by the Spirit with musical ability *encourages* practice and preparation, but *requires* an earnest desire to use that Spirit gift for the glory of God. The Bible *assumes* musical skill and preparation, but *emphasizes* that the motivation and purpose for excellence in worship is to honor and glorify the Lord.

To worship the Lord in spirit and in truth is to be fully aware of God's presence and to approach God in reverence and humility. Worship is not a matter of self-expression but of Word-focused, Christ-centered concentration. There is nothing casual or cavalier about real worship. David's exhortation to "sing joyfully" to the Lord, "play skillfully" and "shout for joy" suggests a range of effort from careful preparation to joyous spontaneity. It takes skill to "make music to [the Lord] on the ten-stringed lyre," and it takes energy to "shout for joy," but neither the preparation nor the enthusiasm of worship was ever meant to obscure the reason for worship. The psalmist is constantly reminding us of why we are worshiping: "Sing to him a new song; play skillfully, and shout for joy. For the word of the LORD is right and true; he is faithful in all he does" (Psalm 33:3–4).

Music must be in tune with the will of God. It is never an end in itself. To say as one disgruntled person said to me, "I worship the music!" is to turn an instrument of praise into an idol. "Unlike the artist who serves the art, we serve the God of the art."[1] C. S. Lewis reminds us that the beauty we long for is not found *in* music but *through* music. Music expresses the longing for what we really desire, but if music is "mistaken for the thing itself," we will turn it into a dumb idol.[2] There is an ever-present danger that the most beautiful music may be out of tune with God's will (Daniel 3:5–10; Revelation 18:22). This was certainly true when Aaron promoted "a festival to the LORD" (Exodus 32:5) and dedicated the golden calf with singing and dancing (vv. 18–19). It was also true during the days of the prophet Amos when the Lord refused to listen to Israel's worship. "Away with the noise of your songs! I will not listen to the music of your harps" (Amos 5:23). Amos, too, was not impressed with the worship, saying, "You strum away on your harps like David and improvise on musical instruments" (6:5). They may have sung and played with King David's musical skill, but they didn't have his heart for God. Instead of grieving over their sorry spiritual state, they were filled with pride.

The prophet Ezekiel faced a similar problem. His messages were well received and his word-of-mouth reputation generated excitement. But people were not listening for God's revelation; they were listening for their own enjoyment and entertainment. They saw Ezekiel as "nothing more than one who sings love songs with a beautiful voice and plays an instrument well, for they hear your words but do not put them into practice" (Ezekiel 33:32). There is a serious problem when worship music is listened to more for its melody than its theology and when the sermon inspires people like a love song.

We forget the struggle the Reformers faced in advocating for worship to be sung and spoken in the language of the people. John Calvin insisted on singing the Psalms in the vernacular so that people wouldn't be murmuring among themselves without any understanding. He also insisted on the exclusive use of the Psalms in congregational singing. Indeed, his concern was so great that worship be rooted in the Word of God that the only source he accepted for lyrics was the Psalms. "When we have looked thoroughly everywhere and searched high and low, we shall find no better songs nor more appropriate to the purpose than the Psalms of David which the Holy Spirit made and spoke through him."[3]

Above all else we want our worship to be in tune with God's will and to proclaim the Gospel of Christ with integrity.

Martin Luther did not share Calvin's strict limitation of congregational singing to the Psalms, but he did share Calvin's conviction to root worship in the Word. Luther wrote a total of thirty-seven hymns. His most famous hymn, *A Mighty Fortress Is Our God,* was written in 1527 after learning that Leonhard Kaiser, a close friend, had been burned at the stake in the Netherlands for refusing to recant. The hymn is based on Psalm 46 and is typical of Luther's reliance upon strong words and a "one syllable, one note" style of composition.[4] Luther believed that the gift of language and the gift of song were given so that we should praise God with both word and music. For Luther, the true use of music was "to the glorification of God and the edification of man." Luther wrote:

> We want the beautiful art of music to be properly used to serve her dear Creator and his Christians. He is thereby praised and honored and we are made better and stronger in faith when his holy Word is impressed on our hearts by sweet music.[5]

Concern for the integrity of God's Word made John Newton, the composer of *Amazing Grace,* suspicious of a beautiful melody. He feared that music could obscure the message of God. Newton conceded that on this side of eternity that

Handel's *Messiah* "executed in so masterly a manner, by persons whose hearts, as well as their voices and instruments, were tuned to the Redeemer's praise; accompanied with grateful emotions of an audience duly affected with a sense of their obligations to his love; might afford one of the highest and noblest gratifications, of which we are capable in the present life."[6] But Newton went on to reason that "true Christians, without the assistance of either vocal or instrumental music, may find greater pleasure in a humble contemplation on the words of Messiah, than can be derived from the utmost efforts of musical genius."[7]

Newton was concerned that people who held the Gospel of the grace of God in contempt could listen to the Messiah with appreciation! "It is to be feared," he wrote, that those "who have received pleasure from the music of the Messiah, have neither found, nor expected, nor desired to find, any comfort from the words."[8] The sensitivities of Newton alert the believer to issues far greater than musicianship when it comes to worship music. Above all else we want our worship to be in tune with God's will and to proclaim the Gospel of Christ with integrity.

THE INDWELLING WORD OF GOD

The apostle Paul concentrated exclusively on the character of the church's music ministry. He said nothing about musicality, but he said much about spirituality. He did not debate musical styles, but he spoke directly to the thought life, moral character, and body life of the household of faith. Against a false model of self-imposed worship (Colossians 2:23), he called for holy living. He began with a grave concern for believers, warning them not to be deceived by a false spirituality that lacked "any value in restraining sensual indulgence" (v. 23), and he ended with the positive admonition to "sing psalms, hymns and spiritual songs with gratitude in your hearts to God" (3:16). In between Paul offered forceful spiritual direction. He challenged believers to "set [their] minds on things above, not on earthly things. For you died, and your life is now hidden with Christ in God" (vv. 2–3). He called them to "put to death" their sin nature and to get rid of sexual immorality, impurity, lust, greed, anger, rage, malice, and slander (vv. 5–8). In short, he insisted that they "put off" the old self with its sinful practices and "put on the new self, which is being renewed in knowledge in the image of its Creator" (Ephesians 4:22; Colossians 3:10). He offered a powerful grace-filled prescription for excellence in music ministry.

The apostle Paul did not envision choir robes for this music ministry. He expected the congregation to be robed in "compassion, kindness, humility, gentleness and patience" (v. 12). Before they could sing in harmony, they needed to live in harmony; before they could sing the melody of love, they needed to practice love. They needed to "let the peace of Christ rule in [their] hearts" if they expected to sing from the heart (v. 15). By the time Paul addresses the ministry of music he has covered the whole range of "Christian graces to be found among God's chosen people and especially their culmination in love, unity, peace and thankfulness."[9] Christian musician Nolan Huizenga is rightly impressed: "What a setting for musical advice! Imagine what a mutuality of these graces among believers could do for the music in our churches!"[10]

The impact of the indwelling Word of Christ is expressed in two parallel clauses: "Let the word of Christ dwell in you richly *as you teach and admonish one another with all wisdom, and as you sing psalms, hymns and spiritual songs with gratitude in your hearts to God"* (v. 16, italics added). Paul emphasized several important truths that help shape our understanding of worship music. *First,* when Paul's admonition in Colossians is combined with his spiritual direction in Ephesians, we see that the inspiration for worship music is by both the filling of the Holy Spirit and the indwelling of the Word of Christ. There is no separation between the Spirit of God and the Word of God.

Second, the impact of the indwelling Word of Christ is experienced in two specific ways, teaching with all wisdom and singing with gratitude in our hearts to God. This twofold expression underscores the close relationship between proclamation and praise in our worship. Both teaching and singing are based on the Word of God.

Third, it is reasonable to conclude that there is a dynamic in spiritual growth: the more we let the Word of God shape us from the inside out, the more our teaching and singing will help us to internalize the Word of God in our lives. To sing the Word with gratitude in our hearts to the Lord is to let the Word into our lives in deeper, more soul-searching, life-transforming ways.

Fourth, when Paul referred to three types of musical expression, "psalms, hymns and spiritual songs" (v. 16), he meant to encourage variety and flexibility in worship music. Most scholars agree that it is not possible to come up with tight definitions and categories for these three terms, because their meanings overlap. Their common purpose is for the praise and adoration of the living God. Paul's intent was not to limit worship music but to allow for "the full range of singing which the Spirit prompts."[11] He would not have agreed with Calvin's conclusion that singing should be based exclusively on the Psalms. Paul ignored issues of musical style, form, and accompaniment and focused on the heart of worship.

Fifth, Paul repeatedly stressed that joy and gratitude are the underlying emotions behind our worship in song. If our hearts are right with God, our voices will sing praise to God. If the peace of Christ is ruling in our hearts and the Word of Christ is dwelling in us richly, it will be impossible to keep us from singing.

Sixth, all believers were meant to participate in singing psalms, hymns, and spiritual songs with gratitude in their hearts to the Lord. "One feels in these verses a kind of 'musical koinonia,' a sense of sharing and active participation by the congregation. The privilege of singing belongs to the whole Christian community, not an elite few."[12]

7

STUDY THE WORD

Do your best to present yourself to God as one approved,
a workman who does not need to be ashamed
and who correctly handles the word of truth.

2 TIMOTHY 2:15

A good friend of mine, Peter Barnes, identifies with the Ethiopian encountered by Philip in the book of Acts. Peter's first serious study of the Bible began in college when he was invited to join a small group. Like the Ethiopian official, Peter needed someone to explain the Word of God to him so that he could understand what he was reading. Luke's description in Acts of one of the first small group Bible studies following the Resurrection highlights an experience that many have had as they have sought to understand the Bible.

Philip was led by the Lord to leave Jerusalem and head for Gaza. On his way, he met an Ethiopian official in charge of finance who was returning from Jerusalem after worshiping at the temple. Once again the Holy Spirit prompted Philip, saying, "Go to that chariot and stay near it" (Acts 8:29). Philip obeyed, and as he neared the chariot he heard the man reading Isaiah the prophet. He was reading from Isaiah 53:7–8, which Acts quotes:

> He was led like a sheep to the slaughter,
>> and as a lamb before the shearer is silent,
>> so he did not open his mouth.
> In his humiliation he was deprived of justice.
>> Who can speak of his descendants?
>> For his life was taken from the earth.
>>>>> (Acts 8:32)

In spite of their obvious social class differences, Philip interrupted the reading with a question. "Do you understand what you are reading?" The Ethiopian responded, "How can I, unless someone explains it to me?" and then he invited Philip to join him in his chariot. He asked Philip, "Tell me, please, who is the prophet talking about, himself or someone else?" The Ethiopian was humble, expectant, and ready to learn, qualities that made him receptive to Philip's insight. Luke summarizes what happened next in a line, "Then Philip began with that very passage of Scripture and told him the good news about Jesus" (vv. 30–35).

If Philip had been a biblical scholar, he might have started with the scholarly debate over the book of Isaiah's authorship or discussed the role of the prophets in Israel's history. Such issues are important and have their place, but they would have sidetracked this critical opportunity. Philip wisely began with "the good news about Jesus," who is clearly the subject of this text and the fulfillment of Isaiah's prophecy. Instead of raising peripheral issues and going down an intellectual alleyway, Philip discussed God's great salvation history story. He told him "the good news about Jesus." The Ethiopian's eager desire

The habit of meeting together provides an added incentive for studying the Word.

to be baptized is a clear testimony of his acceptance of Philip's message and his commitment to

Christ. Luke deftly describes an encounter that went well beyond a religious dialogue or an intellectual discussion. It was a life-changing experience, as all good Bible studies should be.

SMALL GROUP BIBLE STUDIES

Many have found it easier to understand the Word by being able to dialogue and ask questions of sincere believers. Not only does the habit of meeting together provide an added incentive for studying the Word, which we might not have if left to ourselves, but also our understanding of God's Word is deepened as we study and discuss the Bible with believers who share a strong desire to know the Word of God. The importance of small group Bible studies has been stressed throughout the history of the church. Philipp Spener, a seventeenth-century German Pietist, in his classic work *Pia Desideria*, written in 1675, offered many of the same reasons for small groups that we hear today.

Preaching alone, Spener reasoned, did not provide sufficient opportunity to grasp the meaning of the whole counsel of Scripture. There are just not enough Sundays in the year to do justice to the Bible. Spener wrote, "If we put together all the passages of the Bible which in the course of many years are read [and expounded] to a congregation in one place, they will comprise only a very small part of the Scriptures which have been given to us."[1] Spener concluded that the solution was not to be found in private Bible reading: "Although solitary reading of the Bible at home is in itself a splendid and praiseworthy thing, it does not accomplish enough for most people," because "nobody is present who may from time to time help point out the meaning and purpose of each verse."[2]

What he proposed was "to reintroduce the ancient and apostolic kind of church meeting," a small group Bible study led by a knowledgeable mentor. Believers could then "fraternally discuss each verse in order to discover its simple meaning and whatever may be useful for the edification of all." Spener explained, "Anybody who is not satisfied with his understanding of a matter should be permitted to express his doubts and seek further explanation." For Spener, small Bible study groups gave people "a splendid opportunity to exercise their diligence with respect to the Word of God and modestly ask questions (which they do not always have the courage to discuss with their minister in private) and get answers to them."[3] In addition to public preaching and private reading, small groups helped fulfill the admonition of Paul to "Let the word of Christ dwell in you richly, as you teach and admonish one another with all wisdom" (Colossians 3:16). Spener was very hopeful. "If we succeed in getting the people to seek eagerly and diligently in the book of life for their joy, their spiritual life will be wonderfully strengthened and they will become altogether different people."[4]

This episode demonstrates three important benefits of a small group Bible study.

When I was a teenager my family hosted a Bible study for Chinese students from the University of New York at Buffalo. My brother had become friends with several Chinese Christians, and when they needed a place to hold their weekly Bible study, he offered our home. The group began with thirteen students, but it quickly grew to over fifty. Every Friday night they split up into separate language groups—Mandarin, Cantonese,

Hakka, and English—for their Bible studies. The fellowship and food attracted many students unfamiliar with the Christian faith and the Bible.

I remember one student from Taiwan, Wang Hsiao Ming, who came early one week and had dinner with our family before the rest of the group arrived. After the meal, we passed out Bibles for a short reading. "So this is the Bible," Wang remarked, adding that it was the first time he had held a Bible in his hands. Before the year was out, he had become a strong believer. We know of fourteen Chinese students who over time came to know Christ and many more who grew in their faith through this weekly Bible study time. It would be difficult to overestimate the value these small group Bible studies played in transforming people's lives.

Another important illustration in the book of Acts of the value of small group Bible studies is found in the experience of Apollos at Ephesus. Luke describes Apollos as "a learned man, with a thorough knowledge of the Scriptures," who spoke "with great fervor and taught about Jesus accurately, though he knew only the baptism of John" (Acts 18:24–25). He boldly proclaimed a gospel message of repentance and expounded on

the teachings of Jesus, but he was apparently unaware of the outpouring of the Spirit of Christ at
Pentecost and the importance of being baptized
in the name of the Father and of the Son and of
the Holy Spirit (Matthew 28:19). When Priscilla
and Aquila, a missionary couple whom the apostle Paul had left in Ephesus, heard Apollos'
teaching, they "invited him to their home and explained to him the way of God more adequately"
(Acts 18:26).

This episode demonstrates three important
benefits of a small group Bible study. *The first
benefit was the setting.* Instead of challenging and
debating Apollos in public, Priscilla and Aquila
invited him to their home. By offering hospitality
and fellowship, they provided a setting con-
ducive to mutual encouragement and spiritual
growth.

*The second benefit was the attitude of mutuali-
ty and equality in Christ.* This encounter is a testimony to Apollos' humility and his readiness to
grow in Christ. Apollos was a native of Alexan-
dria, a leading intellectual center. He was well ed-
ucated, "a learned man" (v. 24), yet he was open
to being instructed by a couple who probably had
less education and influence than he did. Aquila

was from Pontus (Acts 18:2), a coastal region in northern Asia Minor on the Black Sea. It was a remote place far from the influence of Greek and Roman culture. Apart from Christ, Apollos and Aquila may have had little in common, educationally or otherwise, but in Christ they had much in common and a great deal to discuss.

The third benefit was the principle that we are not alone in our interpretation and understanding of God's Word. Apollos was not out to establish his own version of Christian teaching, nor did Priscilla and Aquila seek to conform Apollos to their way of thinking. They were not competing against one another but seeking to understand and obey the truth of Christ. This led to Priscilla and Aquila's quietly taking the initiative and Apollos' humbly accepting their expla-

> *The principle of sola scriptura, was never intended to make the Bible subject to everyone's private interpretation.*

nation. This particular Bible study proved especially significant because Apollos went on to help many others. Luke writes that Apollos was "a great help to those who by grace had believed.

For he vigorously refuted the Jews in public debate, proving from the Scriptures that Jesus was the Christ" (Acts 18:27–28).

SOLA SCRIPTURA

The sixteenth-century Reformers affirmed the watchword *sola scriptura,* or "only Scripture," in order to stress that the Bible was the undisputed, fully reliable source for understanding and obeying God. They sought to lift the burden of imposed, man-made traditions from Christian practice and to willingly submit to the clearly revealed will of God. They were confident that the content of biblical truth was accessible and understandable to believers. In arguing the point with Erasmus, Luther wrote, "I certainly grant that many passages in the Scriptures are obscure and hard to elucidate, but that is due, not to the exalted nature of the subject, but to our own linguistic and grammatical ignorance; and it does not in any way prevent our knowing all the *contents* of Scripture. For what solemn truth can the Scriptures still be concealing, now that the seals are broken, the stone rolled away from the door of the tomb, and that greatest of all mysteries brought to light—that Christ, God's Son, became man, that God is Three in One, that Christ suffered for us, and will reign for ever?"[5]

Luther reasoned that "the entire content of the Scriptures has now been brought to light, even though some passages which contain certain unknown words remain obscure."[6] It was for this reason that the Reformers championed putting the Bible in the hands of the people and freely proclaiming the Scriptures everywhere.

However, the principle of *sola scriptura,* with its corresponding conviction in the clarity and simplicity of the biblical message, was never intended to make the Bible subject to everyone's private interpretation. The principle of *sola scriptura* is different from the maxim "the

We were meant to prayerfully hear the Bible in the fellowship of God's people.

Bible—and the Bible alone—is good enough for me." The former is said by those who respect and submit to the truth claims of the Bible; the latter is said by those who want to subject the Bible to their individual interpretation and opinion. The Reformation principle affirms the importance of the body of Christ and the community of God's people for understanding and biblical interpretation, whereas the other notion defends private interpretation and personal opinion.

To argue that the Bible is clear, straightforward, and forthright in its message is very different from saying that people can bend and distort it into any shape that suits their purposes. Anyone can make the Bible say whatever he wants it to say as long as he doesn't care about what the Bible really says! Luther argued that it is easy to "throw many passages together helter-skelter, whether they fit or not" and seek to prove virtually anything.[7] John Calvin framed the issue this way: "I acknowledge that Scripture is a most rich and inexhaustible fountain of all wisdom; but I deny that its fertility consists in the various meanings which any man, at his pleasure, may assign."[8] If we are not careful, our passion for the Bible can be cut off from the book itself. That what we love about the Bible is not what's in the pages but what we can make of what's in the pages.[9]

Sola scriptura means *I'm committed to believe and follow what the text of the Bible says,* but "No Creed but the Bible" says in effect, *I believe what*

I want to believe about the Bible without accepting the wisdom of the church and practicing valid principles of interpretation. Sola scriptura is foundational to our life together in Christ, but "the Bible alone" often leaves individuals alone to interpret the Bible on their own.

Just as the Lord sent Philip to the Ethiopian official to help him understand the prophecy of Isaiah in the light of Christ, so the Lord sends us brothers and sisters in Christ to help us interpret God's Word. The principle remains the same whether we are speaking of family devotions, small group Bible studies, or seminary classes. We are not left alone to arrive at our own conclusions about what the Bible teaches. We were meant to prayerfully hear the Bible in the fellowship of God's people, with the earnest desire to obey what we learn from God's Word. Some of the questions may be different at a small group Bible study than in a seminary classroom but the purpose remains essentially the same: "Concentrate on doing your best for God, work you won't be ashamed of, laying out the truth plain and simple" (2 Timothy 2:15, THE MESSAGE).

Humility, wisdom, and the leading of the Holy Spirit encourage us to use the many resources available to us in the body of Christ in order to interpret and apply the Word of God accurately. These resources include biblical commentaries, theological works, Christian books, Bible classes, small group Bible studies, biblical preaching, worship music, special conferences, and seminary classes. All of these resources can be used by the Holy Spirit to help us hear the Word of God with our hearts and our minds and encourage us to apply the truth in our lives. We are not left to ourselves to come up with our own private interpretation of the Bible, nor are we free from the responsibility

Before we can explore the **significance** *of the text we need to understand what the text means.*

to test our sources to see if they are consistent with what the Bible teaches. Like the Bereans, who received the Gospel message "with great eagerness and examined the Scriptures every day to see if what Paul said was true" (Acts 17:11), we have a responsibility to weigh all perspectives in the light of God's Word. May we hold to the truth as they did.

What happens when we combine the princi-

ple of *sola scriptura* with the practical method of
small group Bible studies? This is where we may
run into problems because of the unyielding nature of the Word of God and the prevailing feeling among many that everyone in a Bible study is
entitled to his own opinion. We quickly learn that
Bible study is not fun! At least not in the sense of
a recreational hobby or a leisure time activity.
Hardly an excuse for fellowship, Bible study is a
serious, life-threatening experience. And the life
it threatens is the life based on selfish pursuits,
religious pride, and the spirit of the times.

"The Bible is without question one of the
most unsatisfying books ever written," wrote
Thomas Merton, the famous Roman Catholic
writer and monk. "It is the nature of the Bible to
affront, perplex and astonish the human mind.
Hence the reader who opens the Bible must be
prepared for disorientation, confusion, incom-
prehension, perhaps outrage."[10] Merton's description is accurate as long as we stay with a
make it say what I want it to say mind-set. To
approach the Bible as a self-help tool or as an
inspirational spiritual guide is to experience
frustration, embarrassment, and defensiveness,
because the Bible is constantly eroding our

expectations. To handle the Bible as a medium for self-expression and personal opinion is to feel the constant need of having to do damage control. It is when we receive the Bible as God's Word, a radical word that does not conform to our expectations, that we no longer feel the burden to put a positive spin on the Bible. It is only as we open ourselves up to the Word that we find the Bible to be the most satisfying book ever written, "able to make [us] wise for salvation through faith in Christ Jesus" (2 Timothy 3:15).

HANDLING THE WORD OF TRUTH

Philip's simple question to the Ethiopian, "Do you understand what you are reading?" (Acts 8:30) deserves our attention. It is such an obvious question that we might easily overlook its significance. But to take it for granted is to forget that it is *the* question that focuses all good Bible study. To miss this question is to move beyond the biblical text and bypass what the Bible says. Philip's question focuses on the *meaning* of the biblical text. We are reminded that before we can explore the *significance* of the text we need to understand what the text means.

Bible studies that quickly jump to the question, "What does it mean to you?" before answering the question, "Do you understand what you are reading?" usually end up reflecting the feelings of the reader rather than the meaning of the text. Anyone who has had any experience in small group Bible studies has probably been exposed to the common pitfall of using the Bible as an "ice-breaker" for airing personal concerns and feelings. When "what's on my heart" takes precedence over "what's in the text," so-called Bible study becomes a pretense for sharing opinions and debating ideas rather than studying God's Word and learning to obey.

In theory, Christians criticize relativism, the position that claims truth is a matter of subjective opinion rather than objective revelation, but in practice, Christians often react to the Bible subjectively. They ignore the message of the Bible and focus on how they feel. Rob Suggs' caricature of a small group Bible study is closer to the truth than we care to admit. The leader begins, "So Paul says in Philippians 1:14 that because of his *chains,* others have been encouraged. What do you think he means?"

"Oh, I know," someone speaks up. "Paul's writing a letter, right? So this is a *chain* letter, like the one I just got!"

Someone else disagrees, "No, no, you're missing the point! I'm a *chain* smoker, and God is speaking to me through this to tell me I am to encourage other chain smokers!"

A third person boldly chimes in, "Well, it reminds me of that Aretha Franklin song, *Chain of Fools.* Maybe Paul means we're fools for Christ!"

By now the leader is wondering to himself why he volunteered to lead this Bible study. "Um . . . those are . . . very interesting insights," he says, "but do you think Paul could simply be referring to his *prison* chains, in Rome?"

Everyone looks surprised and someone makes an aside comment, "I told you this Bible study wasn't about practical living."[11]

New Testament scholar Walt Russell advises us "to clean up our language when we talk about Scripture. If we want to discuss the *meaning* of the text, then we ask, 'What does this verse or text mean?' If we want to discuss *significance*, then ask, 'What is the relevance or significance of this verse to you?'"[12] Russell's distinction is based on the work of E. D. Hirsch, who defined meaning as that which is represented in the text and intended by the author. The personal impact of that objective *meaning* on the reader he called *significance*. Hirsch argued that "a text cannot be made to speak to us until what it says has been understood."[13] "Permanent meaning is, and can be, nothing other than the author's meaning."[14]

The fact that a scholar should have to argue such an obvious point may strike some as odd, but Hirsch's perspective is actually a radical observation because it flies in the face of "reader-response criticism" and the modern theory that the text has a life of its own. Instead of deriving *significance* from *meaning,* modern interpreters seek to derive *meaning* from *significance.* In other words, the text can mean whatever the reader wants it to mean. Hirsch warns, "As soon as the reader's outlook is permitted to determine what a text means, we have not simply a changing meaning but quite possibly as many meanings as readers."[15]

Reader-response criticism is popular among many university English professors today because it frees the text from the author's expressed meaning and allows the interpreter creative license to come up with an allegedly more relevant understanding of the text. In the tension between the two horizons, the first horizon being the author's worldview and the second horizon being the interpreter's worldview, priority is given to the second horizon. The critical interpretative question is always first and foremost, "What does this text mean to me?" and it follows that there can be no wrong answers, except of course the author's original meaning. In fact the most eccentric and outlandish perspectives often get the most attention.

Correctly handling the Word of Truth requires serious, honest attention to the biblical text.

This approach to the text makes us think of the modern art critic who has been known to take worthless junk and call it art. You may have seen the CBS *60 Minutes* report that mocked the sale of contemporary art at Sotheby's in New York. "A canvas of scrawls done with the wrong end of a paint brush, bearing the imaginative title of Untitled," went for $2,145,000. Three basketballs submerged in a fish tank sold for $150,000. A blank canvas with the word *Rat* repeated three times went for the bargain price of $30,000.[16] What would otherwise be considered junk assumes great monetary value because of the hype of art dealers and the approval of critics.

This is an extreme case of subjective interpretation, but it highlights a philosophy of meaning that spills over into every sphere of life. The temptation is there to make ourselves the arbitrators of meaning and to assign value according to our likes and dislikes. The sixteenth-century Reformers challenged the Pope's authority where they believed it was in conflict with the Word of God. What we have today is far worse, multitudes of little popes, pontificating on what the Bible says to them without any serious concern for what the Bible means to say.

Correctly handling the Word of Truth requires serious, honest attention to the biblical text. This means that we take into consideration everything that helps us interpret what the Spirit-led authors intended to say. Biblical scholars call this common sense approach the historical-grammatical method. It recognizes the language, grammar, context, culture, and history of the text. No one needs to be an expert in these areas in order to read the Bible, but all of these concerns factor into our understanding of what the text means. "The aim of good interpretation is simple: to get at the 'plain meaning of the text.' And the most important ingredient one brings to that task is enlightened common sense."[17] The historical-grammatical method respects the text by acknowledging that the Holy Spirit does not bypass human rationality, questions of language, and historical context, but works through these means to communicate to us.

To illustrate how this common sense method of interpretation works, consider the apostle Paul's admonition to Timothy to be "a workman who does not need to be ashamed and who correctly handles the word of truth" (2 Timothy 2:15). Begin by examining the context of Paul's spiritual direction. Read through his short letter, identifying the main issues on his mind. The more familiar we are with the apostle's life and writings the easier it will be to understand his concerns and his reasoning. It takes only about ten minutes to read through 2 Timothy. Read it aloud to get a sense of the tone and emotion of the text. Make special note of the repeated themes and the flow of logic. Ask questions of the text: What is the nature of the relationship be-

tween Paul and Timothy? How does Paul appeal
to Timothy and what does he ask Timothy to do?
Put yourself in Timothy's shoes. Try to read 2 Timothy as if it were addressed to you, keeping in
mind that you are the pastor at the church at
Ephesus. How does Paul use his own life as a
challenge and an encouragement to Timothy?

When Paul advised Timothy to "keep reminding them of these things" (2 Timothy 2:14), he left
no doubt as to what he wanted Timothy to remember and to teach. The
theme of "reminding" and
"remembering" is interesting to trace throughout
Paul's letter. His emphasis
here is that Timothy's responsibility was not to
speculate about the faith

Serious Bible study can be compared to listening intently to a close friend.

or innovate new teaching. His role was not to
come up with something exciting and enticing
that would "knock the socks off" his listeners.
His calling was to "keep as the pattern of sound
teaching" (1:13) what the apostle Paul had faithfully and sacrificially delivered to him: "Guard
the good deposit that was entrusted to you—

guard it with the help of the Holy Spirit who lives in us" (1:14).

As Paul had done for Timothy, Timothy was to do for others. He was to hand down the legacy of faith to the next generation, regardless of what it might cost him personally. "You then, my son," Paul entreated, "be strong in the grace that is in Christ Jesus. And the things you have heard me say in the presence of many witnesses entrust to reliable [people] who will also be qualified to teach others" (2:1–2). Paul's point was clear and needed no further elaboration, but he delighted in expounding the Gospel: "Remember Jesus Christ, raised from the dead, descended from David. This is my gospel, for which I am suffering even to the point of being chained like a criminal. But God's word is not chained" (vv. 8–9).

It is obvious from Paul's tone that he was agitated over people inside the church who were obstructing the Gospel of Christ through their debates and disputes. He likened the spread of their teaching to gangrene. He named names and specified the false teaching. With a single line, "The Lord knows those who are his" (v. 19), he drew Timothy's attention to a parallel incident in the Old Testament when a group rose up in opposition to Moses and Aaron (see Numbers 16). Like the church at Ephesus, most churches have to contend with "quarreling about words" (2 Timothy 2:14) and the destructive influence of false teaching. It is easy to find churches and denominations that compromise the clear teaching of God's Word to conform to the spirit of the times. Professing believers debate and quarrel about even basic biblical truths. Like Hymenaeus and Philetus, they have "wandered away from the truth" and their influence will "destroy the faith of some" (vv. 17–18). If we need a watchword for the future of our church, and we do, it should be the apostle Paul's affirmation: "The Lord knows those who are his," and, "Everyone who confesses the name of the Lord must turn away from wickedness" (v. 19).

Serious Bible study can be compared to listening intently to a close friend. We want to pay careful attention to what our friend has to say and really listen with our heart as well as our mind. We want to stop talking and give our friend a chance to speak. We don't want to be like the person in a conversation who stops talking only long enough to think of what to say next. Those who listen well know that it is a learned skill, an active labor, requiring self-denial and self-control. "Always talking, never listening, is a blatant self-assertion."[18] This was the problem that Paul identified in his letter to Timothy. "Warn them before God against quarreling about words; it is of no value, and only ruins those who listen" (v. 14).

Instead of listening to God's Word, they were indulging in "godless chatter" (v. 16), speculating about end times, and engaging in "foolish and stupid arguments" (v. 23). It ruined those who listened to it, diverted people from the truth, and gave the devil an opportunity to ensnare believers. Several years ago the *San Diego Union Tribune* reported a blatant if not bizarre case in point. The headline read "Bible-Citing Match Blamed for Slaying."

A man who lost an early-morning Bible quoting contest killed the man who defeated him, police said yesterday. Gabel Taylor, 38, was shot once in the face outside his apartment yesterday. Police are searching for the suspect. . . .

Taylor, a preacher's brother, and the suspect were comparing their Bible knowledge outside an apartment complex, and each quoted a different version of the same passage, police said. The suspect retrieved his Bible and realized he was wrong, witnesses said.[19]

This is an extreme case of handling the Bible without regard for its meaning! But not totally unlike the Pharisees in Jesus' day who diligently studied the Bible and yet called for Jesus' crucifixion (John 5:39).

What is true in friendship is also true in Bible study, for Bible study is an extension of our communion with God. It takes time and energy to listen well. You can tell from a person's body language whether that person is listening to you or not. Whether a person is bored and restless or attentive and receptive is easily apparent. The same holds true for our spiri-

Our goal is not only accuracy but also faithfulness and obedience.

tual "body language." Whether we are serious about Bible study or not is evident in how attentive we are to the text. It would be foolish if we assumed that we knew everything there was to know about a friend, just as it would be foolish if we felt we knew everything we needed to know about the Bible. Real listening to the Word of God engages the heart and mind. On the one hand, we resist an anti-intellectual attitude that balks at careful study, but on the other hand, we oppose an intellectualizing of the faith that reduces the truth to well-articulated ideas. The appearance of listening, whether in friendship or Bible study, is no substitute for the active, demanding work of listening.

Correctly handling the Word of Truth requires that we keep the message of Christ clearly in focus. Our goal is not only accuracy but also faithfulness and obedience. We not only want to understand what the text says but also live out what the text means. We face the danger of becoming so engrossed in the effort of biblical study and entangled in the mechanics of scriptural exegesis that we forget what we are doing. One biblical scholar observed that often "the outcome of biblical studies in the academy is a trained incapacity to deal with the real problems of actual living persons in their daily lives."[20] This is clearly what we don't want to have happen. We want to constantly remember that "the word of God is living and active. Sharper than any double-edged sword, it penetrates even to dividing soul and spirit, joints and marrow; it judges the thoughts and attitudes of the heart" (Hebrews 4:12).

If we are not careful, the best Bible study in the world can turn deadly if we fail to apply the truth we learn and refuse to live under the authority of the Lord Jesus. Eugene Peterson takes a story out of Herman Melville's novel *White Jacket* to illustrate the dilemma. A sailor who suffered from sharp abdominal pain was diagnosed by Dr. Cuticle, the ship's surgeon, as having an acute appendicitis attack. With assistance from the crew, Dr. Cuticle performed an emergency appendectomy on the poor sailor. Not accustomed to very many surgical opportunities, Dr. Cuticle took his time extracting the diseased organ. He was careful to make precise incisions and point out interesting anatomical details to the sailors assisting him. At the beginning, the sailors were amazed at the doctor's skill and knowledge, but their awe quickly turned to dismay. Dr. Cuticle was so lost in his work and absorbed in the fine art of surgery that he failed to notice that his patient had died—and none of the sailors had the nerve to tell him![21]

Correctly handling the Word of Truth is never an end in itself. The purpose of Bible study goes beyond concepts and ideas. It is fundamentally personal, having to do completely with our relationship to the Lord. The Word of God is a unique tool for being and becoming, without rival or competition. It is not so much an instrument of communication as an instrument of communion. Paul challenged Timothy, "Do your best to present yourself to God as one approved, a workman who does not need to be ashamed" (2 Timothy2:15). Our primary purpose for correctly handling the Word of Truth is not ideological but theological. When we study the Word, we are presenting ourselves to God for His approval. We are not trying to meet our felt needs or satisfy our intellectual curiosity or win the respect of others or impress people with our scholarship or anything else. We study God's Word for one reason only—to present ourselves to God for His commendation, so that we need not be ashamed, "rightly dividing the word of truth" (v. 15 KJV).

The very first small group Bible study following the Resurrection was led by Jesus Himself. It was on the road to Emmaus with two discouraged and dismayed disciples. The first thing Jesus did was to draw their attention to the biblical text. "How foolish you are, and slow of heart to believe all that the prophets have spoken! Did not the Christ have to suffer these things and then enter into glory?" (Luke 24:25–26). The second thing He did was to use the text to guide their understanding. "And beginning with Moses and all the Prophets, he explained to them what was said in all the Scriptures concerning himself" (v. 27). As in all good Bible studies, Jesus based His explanation on the text. What they needed then was exactly what we need today, truth based on God's revelation. Finally, the response of these two disciples is the best thing that could be said of a Bible study: "Were not our hearts burning within us while he talked with us on the road and opened the Scriptures to us?" (v. 32). No matter how you translate that last line, it comes out more as an exclamation than a question. May our hearts and minds be moved when the Word of God is opened for us.

8

PREACH THE WORD

Preach the Word; be prepared in season and out of season;
correct, rebuke and encourage—
with great patience and careful instruction.

2 TIMOTHY 4:2

*A*ll that we have said about hearing the Word involves action. When we pray the Word, meditate on the Word, sing the Word, and study the Word, we participate with the Holy Spirit in taking in the intelligible revelation of God. People who actively listen to the Word want to hear the Word preached when they come to church. They do not want to hear about the latest self-help strategy or be entertained by amusing anecdotes; they want to hear the Word of God in the fellowship of God's people.

God intended for us to hear the Word *together*

through preaching. The apostle Paul's charge to Timothy was emphatic, "Preach the Word." All previous commands, such as "Keep the pattern of sound teaching" and "Guard the good deposit that was entrusted to you" and "Correctly handle the word of truth," are summarized in this imperative, "Preach the Word." Christians agree that this Spirit-given imperative is just as relevant to us today as it was then. It is beyond debate. Preaching is crucial for both evangelism and edification. "Faith comes from hearing the message, and the message is heard through the word of Christ" (Romans 10:17).

But what is important to the follower of Jesus, to pastor and congregation alike, is considered ridiculous to the world. Paul said outright that preaching "the message of the cross is foolishness to those who are perishing, but to us who are being saved it is the power of God" (1 Corinthians 1:18). He did not say it *may be* foolish or *could be* foolish; he said it *is* foolishness to the world. It is not only the medium of preaching that the world finds foolish but the message itself that is foolishness to the world. "For since in the wisdom of God the world through its wisdom did not know him, God was pleased through the foolishness of what was preached to save those who believe" (v. 21).

Preaching lacks everything that worldly speech finds impressive. It is not clever or entertaining in a worldly sense, nor is it sophisticated and intelligent. It lacks the credibility of secular authority and the popular appeal of celebrity status. Preaching has no voice on Wall Street

Preaching is crucial for both evangelism and edification.

or in Hollywood. It is not authoritative speech at Harvard or Stanford. It is not acceptable in a court of law or in the public press. It is sobering to realize that the world judges *all* preaching just as foolish as the worst possible egocentric, opinionated, unbiblical preaching you've ever heard. The very idea that someone can begin a message by introducing the biblical text with saying, "Listen carefully, this is God's Word," is enough to invite the skeptic to look for the exit. Nevertheless, the imperative remains: "Preach the Word!"

THE IMPERATIVE

I am reminded of this imperative every Sunday morning by Thomas McPhatter, an old and dignified retired United States Navy chaplain, who responds to the preaching of the Word with a well-timed refrain, "Preach, brother, preach!" He marks important points with an "Amen." In his deep, resonating voice he encourages me to preach and the congregation to listen. He draws attention to a Spirit-inspired dialogue between the preacher and the people of God. When this veteran black preacher punctuates the Gospel message with "Teach, brother!" or "Preach!" he is challenging a congregation from the pew to sit up and pay attention.

Such encouragement can also be given quietly by the listener's prayerful expectation and attentiveness to the preaching. Body language is often an indication of how attentive people are. An open Bible, frequent eye contact, and an attentive attitude encourage the pastor to *Preach the Word*.

The apostle Paul is an especially good example of one who obeyed this imperative. Timothy did not have to look any further than his mentor for what it meant to "Preach the Word." In Paul, we have a great example of a preacher, not of an orator, for Paul disqualified himself as a superior communicator. "I did not come with eloquence or superior wisdom as I proclaimed to you the testimony about God" (1 Corinthians 2:1).

He also distanced himself from those who used preaching to advance themselves. "It is true," he admitted, "that some preach Christ out of envy and rivalry" (Philippians 1:15), and *many* others "peddle the word of God for profit," but "in Christ," Paul emphasized, "we speak before God with sincerity, like [people] sent from God" (2 Corinthians 2:17). He shunned all forms of manipulation. "We do not use deception, nor do we distort the word of God. On the contrary, by setting forth the truth plainly we commend ourselves to every [one]'s conscience in the sight of God" (4:2). Paul had the stories and the scars to back up his bottom line: "For we do not preach ourselves, but Jesus Christ as Lord, and ourselves as your servants for Jesus' sake" (v. 5).

The real challenge is to preach the Word in the presence of God the Father, Son, and Holy Spirit.

The apostle Paul obeyed the imperative, "Preach the Word," but how could he do otherwise? As he said, he would rather die than have anyone deprive him of the right to preach the Gospel. "Yet when I preach the gospel," Paul said, "I cannot boast, for I am compelled to preach. Woe to me if I do not preach the gospel!" (1 Corinthians 9:16). Paul felt the power of this imperative in his soul. To preach the Gospel was both his greatest privilege and his greatest obligation. To freely obey this imperative was to be both consumed and fulfilled; it was to be both "poured out like a drink offering" (2 Timothy 4:6) and paraded in "triumphal procession in Christ" (2 Corinthians 2:14).

BEFORE GOD

Paul prefaces this imperative with the preacher's ultimate motivation. "In the presence of God and of Christ Jesus, who will judge the living and the dead, and in view of his appearing and his kingdom, I give you this charge: Preach the Word" (2 Timothy 4:1–2). This is what I find to be both the most encouraging and the most unnerving part of preaching. It is not the presence of the seeker who needs to be befriended who is my greatest challenge, nor the skeptic who needs to be convinced, nor the believer who

needs to be helped, nor the troubled soul who
needs to be comforted, nor the nominal Christian who needs to be challenged, nor the growing
disciple who needs to be taught. No, all of these
people are important, but the real challenge is to
preach the Word in the presence of God the Father, Son, and Holy Spirit.

Paul had a vivid sense of proclaiming the
good news of Jesus Christ before the immediate
presence of God, and so should we! Preaching
was to be done with a sincere awareness of being
in the presence of God. He advised Timothy,
"Warn them *before God* against quarreling about
words" (2 Timothy 2:14, italics added), and he
defended his preaching to the Corinthians, saying, "We speak *before God* with sincerity, like
[people] sent from God" (2 Corinthians 2:17, italics added). Is not the chief end of preaching to
give men and women a true sense of the presence
of God—and lead people to Christ?

If a person attending our Sunday morning
worship service was thought to be of special importance in the eyes of the world we would tend
to forget about ourselves and concentrate on
how that person might respond to the message.
We might pay closer attention to the message if

George W. Bush or Lance Armstrong or Oprah Winfrey were hearing the same message we were. It is doubtful whether anyone would get up and leave or doze off during the sermon. The mere presence of a world figure like the president or a celebrity would change the whole atmosphere.

Of course, to put it this way is to think secularly and imply that the significance of the message is somehow tied to the status of the audience, which it is not! But to think spiritually, as the apostle Paul did, is to be fully aware of the presence of God. It is to be acutely aware that God's presence changes

To please God is to preach the Word with authority, humility, clarity, wisdom, eloquence, and passion.

the whole atmosphere. It means that above all else the preacher seeks to please God. Paul posed a rhetorical question to the Galatians, "Am I now trying to win the approval of [people], or of God? Or am I trying to please [people]? If I were still trying to please [people], I would not be a servant of Christ" (Galatians 1:10). He was confident that they would have to agree that he was not a people pleaser but God's servant. "I want you to know, brothers [and sisters], that the gospel I preached is not something that man made up" (v. 11).

Consider the impact on preaching if every thought were intentionally held *captive* "to make it obedient to Christ" (2 Corinthians 10:5). What if every anecdote, analogy, metaphor, illustration, serious point, humorous story, and practical application were screened by a conscience that earnestly sought God's approval, regardless of human opinion. That is not to suggest that God's approval comes at the expense of effective communication to the seeker, the skeptic, or the believer. On the contrary, to please God is to preach the Word with authority, humility, clarity, wisdom, eloquence, and passion, and thus gain the true hearing we seek. Many will despise the Gospel, no matter how effectively and compassionately it is proclaimed. In fact, the better the Gospel is preached the greater will be the resistance. But many others will be moved, taught, convicted, and persuaded that Jesus Christ is the way, the truth, and the life. Paul's wholehearted longing for God's approval inspired his lifelong commitment to "become all things to all [people] so that by all possible means [he] might save some" (1 Corinthians 9:22). "I try to please everybody in every way,"

Paul affirmed. "For I am not seeking my own good but the good of many, so that they may be saved. Follow my example," he encouraged, "as I follow the example of Christ" (10:33–11:1).

The value of the message lies not in how it makes people feel momentarily but how it shapes people for eternity.

Paul was willing to endure "every sacrifice in order to proclaim the truth," but unwilling "to sacrifice the least bit of the truth."[1] The Danish Christian thinker Søren Kierkegaard rightly understood the relationship between Paul's desire to win people to Christ and the apostle's keen awareness of proclaiming the Gospel before God. Commenting on Paul's words, "Since, then, we know what it is to fear the Lord, we try to persuade [people]" (2 Corinthians 5:11), Kierkegaard wrote:

> Therefore there is absolutely no thought in these words of this selfish or cowardly, fearful craving to win people's approval—as if it were the approval of people which decides whether something is true or not. No, the apostle is revealed

before God when he seeks to win people; therefore he does not want to win them for himself but for the truth. As soon as he sees that he can win them in such a way that they become devoted to him but misunderstand him, distort his teaching, he will straightway keep them at a distance in order to win them. He does not wish to win them in order that he himself should have some advantage, but using every sacrifice, and consequently also the sacrifice of their approval, he wants to win them for the truth—if it is possible for him: it is this which he wants. Therefore the same apostle says elsewhere, ". . . We speak as men approved by God to be entrusted with the gospel. We are not trying to please people but God, who tests our hearts. You know we never used flattery, nor did we put on a mask to cover up greed–God is our witness. We are not looking for praise from people, not from you or anyone else" (1 Thess. 2:4–6).[2]

ETERNAL PERSPECTIVE

Paul prefaces his imperative, "Preach the Word," by stressing the immediate presence *and the eternal perspective of God.* The Gospel is not only proclaimed before God, but it is preached "in view of his appearing and his kingdom" (2 Timothy 4:1). This means that the relevance of what is preached is related to God's coming kingdom rather than present-moment happiness. What is uppermost in the mind of the preacher is not the immediate felt needs of the audience but the eternal needs of the listener who is endowed by God with an immortal soul. All temporal concerns are placed in the context of God's eternal truth and His everlasting kingdom. This is why the value of the message lies not in how it makes people feel momentarily but how it shapes people for eternity.

It is entirely different to craft a sermon for temporal effect rather than eternal impact. If the purpose of a sermon is to be entertaining, informative, and successful in the eyes of a restless audience then certain techniques will be used. Perhaps the preacher will begin with a joke or amusing human interest story to connect with the crowd. The preacher will be especially concerned to make everything in the sermon immediately accessible to the audience. There will be an easy, simple-to-follow flow to the sermon. In many cases the Bible will be referred to but not actually opened and read. It will be used as a catalyst for a sermon that focuses on the thoughts and feelings of the listener. Sermons will cover practical issues, such as "How can I have a happier marriage?" "How can I handle money better?" "How do I make life work for me?" "How can I feel better about myself?"

By design the preacher will seek to impress the listener with his vulnerability and his experience. Sermons will be light and informal, liberally sprinkled with humor and personal anecdotes. Often the personality of the speaker will overshadow the message of Christ, and the truth of the Gospel will be reduced to easy-to-remember bullet points. Oscar Wilde said, "About the worst advice you can give anybody is, 'Be yourself.'" That is especially true for preachers, argues William Willimon. Pastors are *supposed* to have their "hands full proclaiming the gospel, pointing to Christ, telling *the* story; [so] there may not be much time to waste pointing to ourselves, sharing our story. John Wesley loved to counter his preachers' tales of how well they had done in the pulpit by asking them, 'But did you offer Christ?'"[3]

One suspects that this seemingly benign emphasis on the personality of the pastor and on how-to pragmatism may fit Paul's warning to Timothy that the time would come "when [people] will not put up with sound doctrine. Instead, to suit their own desires, they will gather around them a great number of teachers to say what their itching ears want to hear" (2 Timothy 4:3). Conservative Christians tend to think that full-blown doctrinal heresy is the only thing that qualifies as a truth-diverting myth, but what if playing to the audience is just as effective in distracting Christians from the truth?

We will see ourselves as God sees us.

Kierkegaard warned of this problem in 1847, claiming that "everything is done to make everything momentary and the momentary is regarded as everything!—Is not everything done to make the present moment as supreme as possible, supreme over the eternal, over the truth; is not everything done to make the present moment self-sufficient in almost proud ignorance of God and the eternal, so conceited in presumed possession of all truth, so presumptuous in the idea of itself being the discoverer of the truth!"[4]

He lamented the fact that preaching no longer required thinking because people were no longer concerned about the truth. Since people have "neither the time nor occasion to reflect on the truth," they "consequently crave superficiality and half truths." Kierkegaard's outlook was bleak:

> Alas, the time of thinkers seems to be past! The quiet patience, the humble and obedient monotony, the magnanimous abandonment of momentary influence, the infinite distance from the momentary, the love devoted to his thought and his God, which is necessary in order to think one thought: this seems to disappear; it is almost on the way to be a laughing-stock to men. "Man" has again become 'the measure of everything' and completely in the understanding of the moment.[5]

A critique of modern preaching does not in any way excuse pedantic and passionless info-sermons. There is no excuse for boring exegesis and tedious sermonizing that lulls a captive audience to sleep. No one should equate boredom and monotony with correctly handling "the word of truth" (2 Timothy 2:15). Serious thought surely does not preclude creativity, sensitivity, humor, and a true passion for Christ. On the contrary, those who hear the Word of God and are transformed by the power and wisdom of the Holy Spirit will preach with great insight and sensitivity. They will listen carefully to the Word of God and use it to address the fallen human condition with clarity, conviction, and compassion. Such is the power of the revealed Word of God that we will see ourselves as God sees us and understand His redemptive grace that alone can save us. True preachers understand that the passion of preaching comes from the tension in the biblical text between the fallen human condition and God's redemptive provision.

Mark Labberton, pastor of First Presbyterian Church of Berkeley, California, writes, "What better definition of bad preaching is there than 'preaching that occurs when all that is present are human words framing human perceptions.'"[6] On the contrary, what better definition of good preaching is there than the challenge given by the apostle Peter: "If anyone speaks, he should do it as one speaking the very words of God" (1 Peter 4:11). There is no apostolic imperative to preach our words and opinions, but there is a divine imperative to *Preach the Word.* This imperative issues out of the conviction that God has spoken in a definitive self-revelation. The Bible describes this self-revelation in words, helping us to hear the voice of God in Creation and leading us to receive God's redemptive love and mercy revealed in God's great salvation history story. When the apostle charged Timothy to "Preach the Word," he meant the entire Word of God, but he especially meant the Word made flesh, the Living Word, the Lord Jesus Christ. To preach the Word meant only one thing, to preach Christ, not as simplification of the biblical message, but as the powerful summation of the whole counsel of God. "Here is the one Word the world must hear and by it be saved. To this one true, saving Word, all Scripture, by the power of the Spirit, speaks its witness."[7]

The apostle Paul's very first thought and absolute bottom line was to preach Christ. What the apostle Paul said to the believers at Corinth communicates the right attitude and true focus of all good preaching. "When I came to you, brothers [and sisters], I did not come with eloquence or superior wisdom as I proclaimed to you the testimony about God. For I resolved to know nothing while I was with you except Jesus Christ and him crucified. I came to you in weakness and fear, and with much trembling. My message and my preaching were not with wise and persuasive words, but with a demonstration of the Spirit's power, so that your faith might not rest on [human] wisdom, but on God's power" (1 Corinthians 2:1–5).

Paul claimed that he did not speak with "eloquence" or "superior wisdom," but judging from his letters, it would be difficult to deny that he preached with both eloquence and persuasion. Augustine, one of the leading early church fathers, addressed this issue by distinguishing between eloquence based on classical rhetorical conventions and true eloquence flowing naturally from the wisdom of God. Augustine reasoned that whether or not Paul "was guided by the rules of eloquence" didn't matter, because what he said could not have been said in a better way. Whatever skill and style Paul used to communicate was dictated by the message he was led by the Spirit to deliver.

Augustine used Romans 5:2–5 as a case in point: "And we rejoice in the hope of the glory of God. Not only so, but we also rejoice in our sufferings, because we know that suffering produces perseverance; perseverance, character; and character, hope. And hope does not disappoint us, because God has poured out his love into our hearts by the Holy Spirit, whom he has given us." Paul was obviously skilled in "the art of elocution." He knew how to build to a climax and emphasize a truth with a rhetorical exclamation. But he never used art simply for art's sake. His purpose was always to call attention to the truth, not the technique.

Augustine held that the sacred writers communicated with a kind of eloquence suitable to those "who justly claim the highest authority, and who are evidently inspired of God."[8] He could not say whether Paul was guided by the rules of classical rhetoric, but he could definitely say that Paul's God-given wisdom was

> *True preaching issues out of the pastor's character, not his sermon outline.*

"naturally produced . . . and . . . accompanied by, eloquence."[9] It was, in Augustine's words, a case of "wisdom not aiming at eloquence, yet eloquence not shrinking from wisdom."[10] Thus, it is best for us to hear Paul's rejection of eloquence and superior wisdom as an emphatic denial of all forms of artificiality, manipulation, and deception, but by no means a rejection of careful reasoning and skillful communication. Paul was never a crafty, clever communicator, but neither was he an artless, boring communicator. No one could ever use the apostle Paul to excuse preaching that lacked depth and clarity, wisdom and passion. His eloquence was natural, flowing out of the passion of his heart. No wonder he stressed to Timothy, "Be prepared in season and out of season; correct, rebuke and encourage—with great patience and careful instruction" (2 Timothy 4:2).

BE PREPARED

In a single sentence, Paul issues a simple, yet compelling challenge to Timothy, one that by its very nature could never lose its urgency and relevance no matter how long a person had been preaching the Word. Paul said it with such brevity that its scope is apparent only upon reflection. Good preaching is never out of season. Its purpose is always for the building up of the body in Christ, and it should always be done with great care and humility.

Sermon preparation pales in significance to this kind of preparation. Timothy's focus was not meant to be upon preparing talks, so that he had a sermon down for every occasion or so that he could preach on a moment's notice. The preparation that Paul urges has to do with Timothy's deepening and abiding relationship to the Lord. True preaching issues out of the pastor's character, not his sermon outline. Pastors preach who they are. All good preaching issues out of lives embraced and transformed by the message of Christ; everything else is sermonizing.

Educator Parker Palmer's observations about teaching apply to preaching. "Good teaching cannot be reduced to technique; good teaching comes from the identity and integrity of the teacher."[11] Parker writes, "One student could not describe her good teachers because they differed so greatly, one from an-

Preaching should come only after careful listening to the Word of Christ.

other. But she could describe her bad teachers because they were all the same: 'Their words float somewhere in front of their faces, like the balloon speech in cartoons.' Bad teachers distance themselves from the subject they are teaching—and in the process, from their students. Good teachers join self and subject and students in the fabric of life."[12]

The same is true of preachers. There is a great difference between those who are truly shaped by the Word of God from the inside out and those who are performing a sermon. It's not difficult to download great sermons off the Internet, but good material alone does not make for good preaching. Besides the ethical problem of plagiarizing other people's work, the pastor betrays the truth itself by copying good ideas instead of embracing the truth personally.

If each and every believer is to hear the Word through meditation, prayer, study, worship, and practice, how much more should the preacher hear the Word faithfully! Before preaching to the congregation, the pastor must be preached to by the Spirit of Christ; preaching should come only after careful listening to the Word of Christ. To be prepared in season and out of season involves constant listening to the Word of God. P. T. Forsyth emphasized this when he said, "The Bible is the supreme preacher to the preacher."[13] However, this most obvious truth is easily forgotten. "It is an immense irony when the very practice of our work results in abandoning our work," writes

Eugene Peterson. "In the course of doing our work we leave our work. But in reading, teaching, and preaching the Scriptures it happens: we cease to *listen* to the Scriptures and thereby undermine the intent of having Scripture in the first place."[14]

For many pastors, faithfulness is a question of concentration, but for Timothy, it was a question of courage. Timothy did not have the luxury of complacency that drew his attention away from the Word of God as we may. His resolve to preach the Word was threatened by persecution and confrontation. For this reason, Paul admonished Timothy to be vigilant in the timeliness of his preaching, whether "in season and out of season," and in the purpose of his preaching, to "correct, rebuke, and encourage," and in the method of his preaching, "with great patience and careful instruction" (2 Timothy 4:2).

Paul backed up this admonition with the example of his own life. Preaching was not just part of Paul's job description; preaching embodied the very essence of his life and ministry in Christ. He embraced the greatness of the task with his whole being. "We proclaim him, admonishing and teaching everyone with all wisdom, so that we may present everyone perfect in Christ. To this end I labor, struggling with all his energy, which so powerfully works in me" (Colossians 1:28–29). Paul likened preaching to manual labor. "Admonishing and teaching everyone with all wisdom" was hands-on, backbreaking, mind-exhausting, muscle straining labor. Paul chose to describe his labor in blue-collar terms. He compared it to exhausting physical work, commonly associated with farming and construction. Paul was not shy about describing the effort and energy expended to proclaim Christ, but he was well aware that it was the Spirit of Christ that turned his labor of love into eternal value.

9

LIVE
THE WORD

He chose to give us birth through the word of truth, that we might be a kind of firstfruits of all he created. . . . Do not merely listen to the word, and so deceive yourselves. Do what it says.

JAMES 1:18, 22

*E*verything that we have studied about taking in the Word of God has as its goal that we might know God and live the Word. We eat the Word, pray the Word, preach the Word, all for the purpose that we should live the Word. And yet we struggle with simple obedience and consistent faithfulness. The prophet Jeremiah was convinced that a new day was coming for the people of God when they would no longer have to say to one another, "Know the Lord," because everyone would know the Lord (Jeremiah 31:34). "'This is the covenant I will make with the house of Israel,' declares the LORD. 'I will put my law in their minds and write it on their hearts. I will be their God, and they will be my people'" (v. 33).

We know that Jesus established this new covenant through His sacrificial death on the cross. He declared it in effect when He instituted Holy Communion, "This cup is the new covenant in my blood, which is poured out for you" (Luke 22:20). And we know the Spirit of Christ established a new consciousness at Pentecost, when He descended upon the apostles. However, on this side of eternity, many who claim to be under the new covenant do not evidence a new consciousness. They

The church seems to suffer from collective spiritual amnesia.

struggle with practicing basic Christian truth and need to be reminded constantly of what it means to follow the Lord Jesus. Instead of internalizing the Word of God, which is what we would expect if the Lord had written His Word on their hearts and minds, many professing believers seem to have to relearn basic truths over and over again. The experience of a new consciousness in Christ is by no means as automatic as we might have thought. The apostle Paul said that "in Christ" we are "a new creation; the old has gone, the new has come!" (2 Corinthians 5:17). But the old ways die hard, and the new ways struggle to survive.

SPIRITUAL AMNESIA

I feel the constant pressure to encourage the church to know the Lord and to live the Word. How can we keep the truth of God's Word ever before us in a church of our size and diversity when so much correction, rebuke, and encouragement seems to go in one ear and out the other? The church seems to suffer from collective spiritual amnesia.

Basic doctrines about Christ, such as the meaning of His incarnation, the purpose of His death on the cross, and the reality of His bodily resurrection, need constant review so that they are not reduced to inspiring metaphors rather than historical realities. Basic biblical moral commands such as integrity, sexual purity, forgiveness, and compassion for those in need require constant repeating so that they are not easily ignored by the believing community. Our culture abounds in selfishness, greed, abortion, homosexual practice, premarital sex, adultery, abuse, pornography, and all types of indulgences. How often must these sins be preached against and the grace of Christ upheld? When we are inundated with a constant barrage of messages stressing personal autonomy, moral indifference, relativism, and materialism, the believing community must be able to take its stand against that which is false and live according to the Truth. Unless the Word of God is obeyed as the Lord promised, "I will put my law in their minds and write it on their hearts" (Jeremiah 31:33), we cannot prevail against the pervasive lies of the culture.

IMAGES OF LIFE

To live the Word is to internalize the truth of God so that we are transformed from the inside out. This is why the psalmist said, "I have hidden your word in my heart that I might not sin against you" (Psalm 119:11). The followers of Jesus grow to depend upon God's direction. We agree with the description of the righteous person in Psalm 1: "His delight is in the law of the LORD, and on his law he meditates day and night"

(v. 2). The psalmist pictured a true relationship to the Word with the botanical imagery of a tree planted by streams of water, "which yields its fruit in season and whose leaf does not wither" (v. 3).

James began with a biological image to describe our relationship to the Lord, "He chose to give us birth through the word of truth," and then switched to an agricultural image, "[so] that we might be a kind of firstfruits of all he created" (James 1:18). These images recall Jesus' parable of the soils. The seed that fell on the path and the rocky ground didn't take root, but the seed that fell on good soil produced an abundant crop (Matthew 13). The metaphors stress the organic life producing way that the Word of God ought to work in us.

God's Word was never meant to be imposed on people or used by preachers (or anyone else) to browbeat believers into submission. Some people want the preacher to try to shake them up and make them feel a little guilty for their worldliness. They find it therapeutic to be told how sinful they are in a sermon so that they can feel a measure of guilt and an ounce of repentance, but their pattern of disobedience persists in spite of this religious fix. Or, if they don't like such sermons for themselves, they think it's important for an erring brother or sister in the next pew to be confronted with his or her sin. This is not what James meant by receiving the implanted Word, nor what Jesus meant when He said, "If you hold to my teaching, you are really my disciples. Then you will know the truth, and the truth will set you free" (John 8:31–32). Jesus often ended His teaching with the refrain, "He who has ears to hear let him hear," as if to separate those who took His words to heart and those who didn't. We have a choice. We can either embrace God's Word or reject God's Word.

There is a great difference between Christians who live the Word consistently and Christians who think about the Word occasionally.

J. I. Packer reminds us of the privilege it is to receive God's message. The Great Physician of our souls, our Lord Jesus Christ, handles us with loving care but does not shy away from the truth about our diagnosis, prognosis, and treatment.

"Our Lord's therapeutic style," Packer observes,

is communicative from first to last. The Bible, heard and read, preached and taught, interpreted and applied, is both the channel and the content of his communication. It is as if Jesus hands us the canonical Scriptures directly, telling us that they are the authoritative and all-sufficient source from which we must learn both what we are to do to be his followers and also, what He has done, is doing, and will do to save us from the fatal sickness of sin.

Think of the Bible, then, as Jesus Christ's gift to you; think of it as a letter to you from your Lord. Think of your name, written in front of it, as if Jesus himself had written it there. Think of Jesus each time you read your Bible. Think of him asking you, page by page and chapter by chapter, what you have just learned about the need, nature, method, and effect of the grace that he brings, and about the path of loyal discipleship that he calls you to tread. That is the way to profit from the Bible. Only when your reading of the written word feeds into your relationship with the living Word (Jesus) does the Bible operate as a channel of light and life that God means it to be.[1]

There is a great difference between Christians who live the Word consistently and Christians who think about the Word occasionally. This is not a new problem. The seventeenth-century Puritan pastor Richard Baxter made preaching his number one priority and endeavored to preach as plainly and as effectively as he could, but he became frustrated with the spiritual immaturity and indifference of many church-goers. "I frequently meet some of my hearers who have listened to me for eight or ten years and still do not know whether Christ be God or man. They wonder when I tell them of His birth, life, and death. They still do not know that infants have original sin. Nor do they know the nature of repentance, faith, or the holiness required of them. Most of them have only a vague belief in Christ, hoping that He will pardon, justify, and save them. And the world still holds their hearts."[2]

Baxter's concern reminds us of the first-century assessment given by the author of Hebrews, when he lamented the immaturity of believers. "It is hard to explain," he wrote, "because you are slow to learn. In fact, though by this time you ought to be teachers, you need someone to teach you the elementary truths of God's word all over again. You need milk, not solid food! Anyone who lives on milk, being still an infant, is not acquainted with the teaching about righteousness. But solid food is for the mature, who by constant use have trained themselves to distinguish good and evil" (Hebrews 5:11–14).

James was concerned as well. "Do not merely listen to the word," he wrote, "and so deceive yourselves. Do what it says" (James 1:22). He was struck by the paradox that those who were given "birth through the word of truth" (v. 18) lived as if the Word of God meant nothing to them. They should have humbly received the implanted word, but instead they were indifferent to God's Word. The imagery of being birthed and rooted in the Word of God is very different from the image James used to describe the Christian who remains prone to evil and deception. That person is like someone who looks in the mirror and turns away and immediately forgets what he looks like (vv. 23–24). James deliberately chose an illustration that contrasted the superficial

There is a specific, practical way to live the Word when it comes to facing hardships.

experience of seeing yourself in a mirror and the life-changing experience of being born again through the Word of Truth. For James, hearing the Word without living the Word was like glancing at yourself in the mirror. It had no lasting effect. Such exposure to the Word was inconsequential and easily forgotten.

FIVE POINTERS TO KEEP IN MIND

If we agree that Jesus gives us not only a new covenant but a new consciousness because He has written His Word in our hearts, how shall we honor and obey this Word? If we are sensitive to Baxter's complaint and the author of Hebrew's lament, how shall we learn to live the Word? If we are struck by James' contrasting illustrations of essential truth and passing fancy, how shall we humbly receive the implanted Word so that it takes root in our lives?

James gave a short answer and a long answer to that question. The short answer underscores the simplicity of the solution. Believers received a simple, straightforward admonition. "The [person] who looks intently into the perfect law that gives freedom, and continues to do this, not forgetting what he has heard, but doing it—he will be blessed in what he does" (James 1:25). In other words, to quote the Nike tag line, "Just do it."

The long answer underscores the complexity of the solution. The entire letter of James is designed to move believers from complacency and indifference to active obedience and moment-by-moment faithfulness. There is a specific, practical way to live the Word when it comes to facing hardships. The world does not say, "Consider it pure joy . . . whenever you face trials of many kinds" (v. 2), but the Word does. The world does not define significance as looking after orphans and widows in their distress, but the Word does. The world does not advise keeping oneself from being polluted by the world, but the Word does. The world does not reject favoritism nor put a priority on taming the tongue, but the Word does. Everything James had to say focused on the issue of living the Word in a culture that honored ambition over humility, greed over sacrifice, and wealth over wisdom. In the Spirit-led tradition of James, here are five fundamental pointers to keep in mind so that we do what the Word of God tells us to do.

1. *Keep your first love.* Don't let your passion for Christ fade into a religious routine or self-righteous hypocrisy. When Christians allow other passions to compete with their love for Christ, the desire to live for God is seriously affected. James could not have been stronger in his warning: "You adulterous people, don't you know that friendship with the world is hatred toward God? Anyone who chooses to be a friend of the world becomes an enemy of God" (James 4:4). The apostle John said much the same thing, "Do not love the world or anything in the world. If anyone loves the world, the love of the Father is not in him. For everything in the world—the cravings of sinful man, the lust of his eyes and the boasting of what he has and does—comes not from the Father but from the world" (1 John 2:15–16). In the letters to the seven churches, the church in Ephesus was commended for its perseverance and endurance but warned that they had lost their first love. "Remember the height from which you have fallen! Repent and do the things you did at first" (Revelation 2:5).

A passion for Christ should not be confused with misdirected religious zeal or immature spiritualized excesses. Those who live the Word invariably have a richer, fuller life. God leads them into His large grace-filled world. Worldliness invariably leads a person into a smaller, meaner, fragmented, and disoriented world. It is a world of lust, indulgence, selfish pleasure, greed, manipulation, and a host of other issues that hurt the soul, feed the ego, and rob the person of peace. A passion for Christ will embrace the fullness of life. Jesus said, "I have come that [you] may have life, and have it to the full" (John 10:10). This is the rea-

James called believers to accept negative hardship as a positive catalyst for wisdom and maturity.

soning behind James' warning, "Don't be deceived. . . . Every good and perfect gift is from above, coming down from the Father of the heavenly lights, who does not change like shifting shadows" (James 1:16–17). If we keep our first love for Christ, we will embrace everything in life that nurtures beauty, wisdom, and goodness.

2. *Be willing to grow up in Christ.* Much of North American Christianity is oriented toward getting people to become Christians without

giving much attention to helping them grow up in Christ. Many Christians are fed a steady diet of entry-level evangelism. Jesus never made the distinction that is commonly made today between evangelism and edification. In fact, whenever He was evangelizing, He consistently stressed the cost of discipleship. Much of today's evangelism offers cheap grace to get people in the door and then holds the radical life-changing, take-up-your-cross-and-follow-Jesus message until later, if ever. However, if we expect to live the Word, it is important that we understand the Word and seek to apply it. There is no evidence in the New Testament that the apostles tried to produce *admirers* of Jesus. Their only concern was to nurture the *followers* of Jesus. They were motivated to "present everyone grown up in Christ" (Colossians 1:28).[3]

That is why James begins his letter with a basic discipleship directive. "Consider it pure joy . . . whenever you face trials of many kinds, because you know that the testing of your faith develops perseverance. Perseverance must finish its work so that you may be mature and complete, not lacking anything" (James 1:2–4). James called believers to accept negative hardship as a positive catalyst for wisdom and maturity.

In many ways, more hardship would be good for us all. I don't mean the hardships that we bring down upon ourselves because of foolish choices and sinful practices but the hardships that come in the course of life. These hardships can drive us to God and cause us to "grow in the grace and knowledge of our Lord and Savior Jesus Christ" (2 Peter 3:18). I know that this has been true in my own life; hardship has played a role in helping me grow in Christ.

The prophet Micah asked a question that is good for us to ask: "What does the Lord require of [us]?" (v. 8). He asked that question to counter the extravagant and grandiose suggestions that were coming from the religious culture. Micah spoke sarcastically of those who were trying to impress God with their religious sacrifices. The prophet pointed to a more concrete, earthy spirituality. There was no mystery to God's requirements. They were uncomplicated and plain for all to understand. "He has showed you . . . what is good. And what does the LORD require of you? To act justly and to love mercy and to walk humbly with your God" (Micah 6:8). If it is our purpose to accomplish these three goals—to act justly, to

love mercy, and to walk humbly with our God—
there is no question that we will grow up in Christ.

3. *Since you live in the Spirit, then walk in the
Spirit.* If we have a passion for Christ and if it is
our purpose to grow in Christ, then we will want
to follow the Lord in practical, Spirit-directed
ways. We will accept the spiritual direction that
says to us, "Live by the Spirit, and you will not
gratify the desires of the sinful nature" (Galatians 5:16). Instead of doing the acts of the sinful
nature, which Paul claimed were obviously
wrong, we will endeavor to practice the fruit of
the Spirit. When Paul said, "Those who belong to
Christ Jesus have crucified the sinful nature with
its passions and desires" (v. 24), he was not
speaking piously, but practically. "Since we live
by the Spirit," Paul reasoned, "let us keep in step
with the Spirit" (v. 25). From this conviction
flows the daily, practical desire to live the Word.

Recently I taught a theology course on how
God shapes us through relationships. It was a
graduate level course and I worked hard to ex-
amine what the Bible says about a number of
important issues, such as self-understanding,
personal wholeness, friendship, sexuality, single-

ness, marriage, and parenting. My aim was to explore these issues in the light of the Word of God and in tension with prevailing ideas in culture. Although I am experienced in academic theology and philosophical reasoning, I found this course particularly challenging. The concepts that lie behind a soulful strategy to follow God-honoring relationships may sound simple, but they are by no means simplistic and are all too rarely integrated into our lives in a personal and practical way.

If I had taught this course years ago, when I was teaching in a seminary full-time, I would have undoubtedly been more theoretical in my lectures and inclined to intellectualize the subject. My rhetoric would have sounded more academic, and the issues would have been covered in a more philosophical manner. I would have employed a scribal approach that quoted heavily from this or that expert or scholar. After nearly twenty years of being a pastor, I realize that the greater challenge in a theology class is not figuring out what the teacher is trying to say but trying to clearly understand and apply the Word of Truth to daily life.

Many of the students responded very positively,

but I was surprised at the reaction and attitudes of a few students who dismissed the material as too simplistic and basic. They let me know that as far as they were concerned the material was relevant for young Christians but beneath them intellectually. I struggled with this assessment, because I felt I was working at the limit of my theological and pastoral understanding on the subject. It struck me as ironic. These students probably would have respected me more when I was a rookie teacher, but now that I'm trying to wrestle with the practical implications of what it means to live for Christ in the matrix of our relationships, I sounded too simplistic and pious.

4. *Learn to identify and resist the strategies of self-deception.* The natural desire for a Spirit-led believer is to become increasingly sensitive to the ways life becomes co-opted by sin. Søren Kierkegaard said that becoming aware of our own sin is like trying to see our own eyeball. Sensitivity to our spiritual blind spots and our moral passivity is not an easily acquired skill. The sin that so easily entangles does not loosen its grip without a struggle. Fallen human nature is inclined to pacify and placate the conscience. We are prone to think

favorably of ourselves and suspiciously of others. We tend to take pride in our righteous acts and overlook our sin. We substitute good intentions for good actions. C. S. Lewis observed that when we are getting better, we understand more and more clearly the evil that is still in us, but when we are getting worse, we understand our own badness less and less. "To learn to detect the same real inexcusable corruption under more and more of its complex disguises, is therefore indispensable to a real understanding of the Christian faith."[4]

James didn't sugarcoat his words. "Submit . . . to God. Resist the devil, and he will flee from you. Come near to God and he will come near to you. Wash your hands, you sinners, and purify your hearts, you double-minded. Grieve, mourn and wail. Change your laughter to mourning and your joy to gloom. Humble yourselves before the Lord, and he will lift you up" (James 4:7–10). It is hard to imagine anyone who followed this spiritual direction not becoming more sensitive to his sin. Who wouldn't become more conscious of how they used their tongue and their wealth? We pray as the psalmist prayed, "Search me, O God, and know my heart; test me and know my anxious thoughts. See if there is any offensive way in me, and lead me in the way everlasting" (Psalm 139:23–24).

5. *Surround yourself with people who love the Word of God and seek to obey it.* A final encouragement to live the Word is found in the fellowship of those who "let the word of Christ dwell in [them] richly" as they "teach and admonish one another with all wisdom, and as [they] sing psalms, hymns and spiritual songs with gratitude in [their] hearts to God" (Colossians 3:16).

Good exegesis is no substitute for faithful obedience.

This is a very special like-mindedness that should not be confused with a typical religious gathering. We should be just as wary of group selfishness as we are of individual selfishness. Groups, even church groups, can demand that we sacrifice "the God-relationship in order to unite in a worldly way."5 When God is locked out of the group or brought along "for the sake of appearance," Christians are worse off than if they stood alone. This is not the kind of group that encourages us to live the Word. But where the fellowship is centered in Christ and the Bible is studied honestly and seriously, we find great encouragement to hold to the hope we profess, and we can spur one another on to love and good deeds (Hebrews 10:23–24).

Dietrich Bonhoeffer wrote, "The more genuine and the deeper our community becomes, the more will everything else between us recede, the more clearly and purely will Jesus Christ and his work become the one and only thing that is vital between us."[6] It is in this community—the body of Christ—that we do not live "by our own words and deeds, but only by that one Word and Deed which really binds us together—the forgiveness of sins in Jesus Christ."[7]

There is much that could be said about living the Word, but the bottom line remains simple. James summed it up when he said, "Therefore, get rid of all moral filth and the evil that is so prevalent and humbly accept the word planted in you, which can save you" (James 1:21). Our main obstacle to doing the will of God is not intellectual or conceptual. Good exegesis is no substitute for faithful obedience. We don't want "to merely listen to the word, and so deceive [ourselves]" (v. 22). We want to live the Word!

Moses captured what it means to live the Word when he said, "These commandments that I give you today are to be upon your hearts. Impress them on your children. Talk about them when you sit at home and when you walk along the road, when you lie down and when you get up. Tie them as symbols on your hands and bind them on your foreheads. Write them on the doorframes of your houses and on your gates" (Deuteronomy 6:6–9). Those who determine to live the Word in this way will discover that the Lord has put His Word in their minds and written it on their hearts.

10

STAY IN THE WORD

Later, knowing that all was now completed, and so that the Scripture would be fulfilled, Jesus said, "I am thirsty."

JOHN 19:28

*W*hat would it be like for you to live your life in such a way that the Word of God was fulfilled? How would it be if *you*, your self-understanding, your priorities and goals, your work ethic and career choices, your use of money and time, your compassion for others and your conviction of truth, your friendships and relationships, your hopes and desires; that is, everything that is important about you could best be understood in the light of your obedience to the Word of God? And people who knew you knew that about you! In other words, instead of being defined by your genealogy, genes, gender, or generation, you were defined by the Word of God.

If this were true, the Christian business person would be best understood by the kingdom priorities of Jesus rather than the ethos of the corporate culture, and the Christian student would be identified by what Jesus said in the Sermon on the Mount rather than what was coming out of pop culture. Everyone who claimed to follow Jesus would be known by their faithfulness to God and His Word.

We have explored the many ways that followers of the Lord Jesus hold to the intelligible revelation of God. Through worship, prayer, preaching, meditation, study, and obedience we absorb the truth of God's Word into our "bloodstream." It shapes who we are and who we want to become. Those who know the Word through song and proclamation,

Getting started in the Word should come early in our walk with Christ.

personal meditation and practical daily obedience, come to love the Word. They embrace this Word of Truth, not as a religious book, but as the very revelation of God that leads them into communion with their Lord and Savior, Jesus Christ.

The various ways in which we take in God's truth should not be viewed as specialized and separate learning strategies. Each is meant to be an essential part of the believer's daily and weekly experience of the Word. Together they are used by the Spirit of Christ to inform our minds and move our hearts. Those who eat the Word find the energy to obey God's truth. Those who sing the Word have a melody in their hearts to the Lord that focuses the soul like no other song in the world. Those who model the Word take their vision for ordinary living from pages of the Bible rather than the glossy pictures of lifestyle magazines. Those who hear the preached Word live under a mandate of liberty unlike any other political declaration or constitution. These *intentional actions* are as necessary to spiritual growth as good soil, adequate water, and plenty of sunlight are to plant growth. And just as with plants, we need a daily supply in order to grow up in Christ.

Getting started in the Word should come early in our walk with Christ. Hopefully you were encouraged at a young age to take the Word seriously and you felt the power of the Holy Spirit opening up your mind and heart to the meaning of the Word. But even if that challenge did not come early in your life, or if it came early and was ignored, the challenge is before you today. The author of Hebrews entreated, "Today, if you hear his voice, do not harden your hearts" (Hebrews 3:7–8). And the apostle Paul exhorted, "Do not put out the Spirit's fire; do not treat prophecies with contempt" (1 Thessalonians 5:19–20). The purpose of our study has been to help confirm and strengthen our commitment to embrace the Word of God. *Getting started in the Word was meant to be a one-time challenge; staying in the Word is meant to be the daily challenge for as long as our lives shall last.*

OUR BEST EXAMPLE

1. *Growing up in the Word of God.* Jesus is the best example we have for staying in the Word. Every time we encounter Jesus in the Gospels, He was mindful of being in sync with the will of His Father. He was always conscious of fulfilling the Word of God. From His experience in the temple at the age of twelve to His dying breath on the cross, Jesus courageously stayed in the Word.

His example ought to be, and indeed can be the model for our lifelong relationship to the Word of God.

Jesus' relationship to the Father's will was unique. What was said of Jesus as a boy in that temple, "Everyone who heard him was amazed at his understanding and his answers" (Luke 2:47), is not something we expect of seventh graders in our church. But neither should Luke's description of Jesus embracing the Word of God at a young age be dismissed as an impossible expectation for today's young people. Instead of distancing ourselves from this important example on the grounds that Jesus was unique, we ought to welcome it as an encouragement. Young people can receive the truth of God at a young age as Jesus did. They can take it in thoughtfully, intelligently, and practically, not as a subject to be mastered through indoctrination but as the truth that shapes their lives.

There is a great difference between a child's learning biblical facts and memorizing verses and a child's also learning to live life according to God's Word. It is one thing to take a Bible quiz, the way one takes a spelling test at school, and another thing to experience the guidance of

God's Word. Young people who are surrounded by parents and mentors who "work out their salvation with fear and trembling" (Philippians 2:12) will be challenged more readily to seriously consider what the Bible has to say. They will have the advantage of being able to picture what obedience to the Word looks like in real life.

If by the grace of God the challenge to follow Jesus has come to you at a young age, please do not put it off. Don't say to yourself that you have plenty of years ahead of you to get serious about the Word of God. That is a fatal rationalization that will cost you dearly. Older believers will tell you this is true. They have learned the hard way through broken marriages, selfish decisions, and painful career choices the unsatisfying cost of non-discipleship. I have never met a believer who regretted following the Word of God from a young age, but I have met many who wished they had obeyed the Word of God when they were young. Grow up in Christ and experience the difference obedience to the Word of God makes in choosing a career, facing hardships, serving others, and living for Christ and His kingdom. Just as Jesus "grew in wisdom and stature, and in favor with God and men," so can you! (Luke 2:52).

2. *Living out the Word of God.* The way Jesus began His public ministry is the best example we have for how believers in their twenties or thirties should embark on careers. Full of the Holy Spirit, Jesus was led into the wilderness for an encounter with the devil that

Obedience is not complicated.

challenged His identity, His mission, and His relationship with the Father. Satan's three temptations of Jesus represent what is at stake when we are led by the Spirit into the world to fulfill God's calling in our lives. Like Jesus, we face the temptations to satisfy our needs and wants selfishly, to substitute idols for the living God, and to vainly attempt to use God for our own purposes.

In the face of extreme physical weakness, Jesus boldly countered the temptations with the Word of God. Each of the devil's challenges was met decisively with the truth of God. Quoting a line from Deuteronomy 8:3, "Man does not live on bread alone," Jesus refuted the devil's attempt to reduce Him to a self-made man focused on satisfying His needs by whatever means possible (Matthew 4:4).

Jesus responded to the second temptation

with a simple, humble recognition of God's sovereign care over His life. "It is also written: 'Do not put the Lord your God to the test'" (Matthew 4:7; cf. Deuteronomy 6:16).

Finally, Jesus put an end to this series of temptations with a statement that was equally concise and put an abrupt stop to any thought the devil had that Jesus might circumvent the Cross and sabotage the will of the Father. "Away from me, Satan! For it is written: 'Worship the Lord your God, and serve him only'" (v. 10; cf. Deuteronomy 6:13).

There is no time like the present to stay in the Word.

Jesus expressed these basic biblical truths out of the depth of His being. They are not proof texts or magical incantations, but deeply internalized truths, capturing the essence of His devotion to the will of the Father. There is no spiritual calculus behind these statements. Obedience is not complicated. We have at our disposal truths that will protect and deliver us from the temptations that threaten to rob us of our identity, mission, and fellowship in Christ.

Jesus not only showed us what we are up

against when we get a job, go off to university, or begin a career, but He also showed us how to stay in the Word. It would be easy for believers in their twenties and thirties to say to themselves that they would like to try to turn stones into bread for a few short years, and then when they get tired of proving themselves to the world, they will take God seriously. It's easy to rationalize bowing down to the worldly powers for the time being in order to get ahead in the rat race. And there are plenty of Christians who have selfishly put God to the test, only to become disillusioned because God isn't there for their personal peace and prosperity.

If you find yourself in the wilderness, tempted by the devil to surrender your true identity and subvert your real calling, please know this: There is no time like the present to stay in the Word. If you put obedience and faithfulness off to some future date, claiming that things will be different when you have more money or you've achieved a higher position or when the kids are older, chances are that day will never come and you'll live to regret your loyalty to the gods of money, sex, and power. Or, you can stand up to the devil with the powerful truth of God's Word. Isn't this why the apostle Paul advised us to put on the full armor of God, so that when the day of evil comes, we may be able to stand our ground? "Truth, righteousness, peace, faith, and salvation are more than words. Learn how to apply them. You'll need them throughout your life. God's Word is an *indispensable* weapon" (Ephesians 6:14 THE MESSAGE).

However, if by the grace of God this challenge is coming to you and you have not stayed in the Word but fallen for the devil's temptations, you need to know that there is still time to change. The promise holds, "If we confess our sins, he is faithful and just and will forgive us our sins and purify us from all unrighteousness" (1 John 1:9). The wilderness will never change, but with God's forgiveness and strength you can take a stand on the Word of Truth. You will continue to be tempted to change stones into bread to prove yourself. You will continue to be enticed to bow down to the gods of money, sex, and power, but by the grace of God you can overcome evil. Human persuasion alone will fail to keep you in the Word, but the Lord Jesus is faithful and will keep you if you want to be kept! Do you have ears to hear what the Spirit is saying to you?

3. *Fulfilling the Word of God.* The way Jesus ended His earthly ministry is the best example we have for staying in the Word right through to the end. When the apostle John described the final moments before Jesus died on the cross, he offered an assessment that should not be overlooked. "Later, knowing that all was now completed, and so that the Scripture would be fulfilled, Jesus said, 'I am thirsty'" (John 19:28). John drew our attention to the most obvious fact of Jesus' life and death. Jesus lived in such a way as to fulfill Scripture. He intentionally chose a course of action that was obedient to the revealed will of the Father. *Christians have little trouble acknowledging that Jesus was acutely aware of completing a destiny prescribed by the Word of God, but they have a great deal of difficulty seeing themselves as completing their God-given destiny.* We find it hard to believe that Christ calls us to fill up what is still lacking in His suffering, for the sake of the

> *What better epitaph at the end of our earthly life than the consciousness of having completed the will of the Father in obedience to His holy Word.*

church (Colossians 1:24). We tend to reduce faith in Christ to a set of beliefs and behaviors that require adherence and compliance, and forget the fact that God calls us to take up our cross and follow Him. In Christ, we too have a destiny that is to be fulfilled in accordance with the truth of God's Word. The challenge to stay in the Word is a far more dynamic and costly undertaking than we ever imagined.

May what John said of Jesus, as He hung on the cross for our sins and griefs, shape our thoughts and guide our actions: "knowing that all was now completed, and so that the Scripture would be fulfilled . . ." (19:28). What better epitaph at the end of our earthly life than the consciousness of having completed the will of the Father in obedience to His holy Word. I want to live right up to the end so that the Word of God is fulfilled in my life.

NOTES

Chapter 1 *Eat the Word*

1. Rick Richardson, *Evangelism Outside the Box* (Downers Grove, Ill.: InterVarsity, 2001), 48.

Chapter 2 *Meditate on the Word*

1. Dietrich Bonhoeffer, *Meditating on the Word* (New York: Ballantine, 1986), 32–33.

2. Ibid., 31–33.

3. Dietrich Bonhoeffer, *Life Together,* translated by John Doberstein (New York: Harper & Row, 1954), 82–83.

4. J. I. Packer, *Knowing God* (London: Hodder & Stoughton, 1973), 20.

5. Derek Kidner, *Psalms 73–150* (Downers Grove, Ill.: InterVarsity, 1975), 302.

6. Ibid., 305.

Chapter 3   *Pray the Word*

1. John S. Feinberg, *Deceived By God? A Journey Through Suffering* (Wheaton: Crossway, 1997), 33–34.

2. Ibid., 135; italics added.

3. Ibid., 137.

4. Ibid., 137.

5. Brother Lawrence, *The Practice of the Presence of God* (Grand Rapids: Spire, 1967), 26.

6. Derek Kidner, *Psalms 73–150* (Downers Grove. Ill.: InterVarsity, 1975), 123.

7. C. H. Spurgeon, *The Metropolitan Tabernacle Pulpit,* vol. 13 (Pasadena, Tex.: Pilgrim, 1979), 485.

8. Ibid.

9. Ibid., 488.

Chapter 4   *Model the Word*

1. John R. W. Stott, *Christian Counter-Culture: The Message of the Sermon on the Mount* (Downers Grove: InterVarsity, 1978), 122.

2. Lisa Graham McMinn, *Growing Strong Daughters* (Grand Rapids: Baker, 2000), 200.

3. Ibid., 201.

4. Ibid. Mrs. McMinn is quoting her husband.

Chapter 5   *Picture the Word*

1. Derek Kidner, *Proverbs* (Downers Grove, Ill.: InterVarsity, 1964), 36.

2. Kathleen Norris, *Amazing Grace* (New York: Riverhead, 1998), 55.

3. Ibid., 56.

4. Ibid., 57.

Chapter 6   **Sing the Word**

1. Richard D. Dinwiddie, "The God Who Sings," *Christianity Today,* 15 July 1983: 21.

2. C. S. Lewis, *The Weight of Glory* (New York: Collier, 1965), 7.

3. Charles Garside Jr., *The Origins of Calvin's Theology of Music: 1536–1543* (Philadelphia: American Philosophical Society, 1979), 33.

4. Richard D. Dinwiddie, "When You Sing Next Sunday, Thank Luther," *Christianity Today,* 21 October 1983: 19.

5. Ibid., 21.

6. John Newton, *The Works of the Rev. John Newton,* vol. 4, *Messiah: Fifty Expository Discourses,* Sermon I (Edinburgh: Banner of Truth, 1985), 2.

7. Ibid.

8. Ibid., 15.

9. C. Nolan Huizenga, "A Biblical 'Tune-up' for Hymn Singing," *Christianity Today,* 27 June 1980: 21.

10. Ibid.

11. Peter T. O'Brien, *Word Biblical Commentary,* vol. 44, *Colossians* (Waco, Tex.: Word, 1982), 210.

12. Huizenga, "A Biblical 'Tune-up' for Hymn Singing," 22.

Chapter 7 **Study the Word**

1. Philipp Jacob Spener, *Pia Desideria*, translated by Theodore Tappert (Philadelphia: Fortress, 1964), 88.

2. Ibid., 88, 90.

3. Ibid., 89, 90.

4. Ibid., 91.

5. Martin Luther, *The Bondage of the Will*, translated by J. I. Packer and O. R. Johnston, (Old Tappan, N. J.: Revell, 1957), 71.

6. Ibid., 71.

7. Nathan O. Hatch and Mark A. Noll, eds., *The Bible in America* (New York: Oxford Univ. Press, 1982), 61.

8. Ibid.

9. Ann Monroe, *The Word* (Atlanta: Westminster John Knox, 2000), 39–40.

10. Ibid., 209.

11. Rob Suggs, *Christianity Today,* 26 October 1992: 30–31.

12. Walt Russell, "What It Means to Me," *Christianity Today,* 26 October, 1992: 31.

13. E. D. Hirsch, *Validity in Interpretation* (New Haven: Yale Univ. Press, 1967), 210.

14. Ibid., 216.

15. Ibid., 213.

16. CBS News, *60 Minutes,* 19 September 1993.

17. Gordon D. Fee and Douglas Stuart, *How to Read the Bible For All Its Worth* (Grand Rapids: Zondervan, 1982), 16.

18. Walter Wangerin, *As for Me and My House* (Nashville: Nelson, 1987), 166.

19. *San Diego Union Tribune,* 16 July 1996.

20. Walter Wink, as quoted by Anthony Thiselton, *The Two Horizons* (Grand Rapids: Eerdmans, 1980), 86.

21. Eugene H. Peterson, *Working the Angles: The Shape of Pastoral Integrity* (Grand Rapids: Eerdmans, 1987), 74.

Chapter 8   Preach the Word

1. Søren Kierkegaard, *Works of Love,* translated by Howard Long and Edna Long (New York: Harper & Row, 1962), 336.

2. Ibid.

3. William H. Willimon, "Naked Preachers Are Distracting," *Christianity Today,* 6 April 1998: 62.

4. Kierkegaard, *Works of Love,* 337–38.

5. Ibid., 338.

6. Mark Labberton, "Glorious Foolishness," *Leadership,* Winter 2000: 32.

7. Ibid.

8. Augustine, "On Christian Doctrine," Book 4:6, *Nicene and Post-Nicene Fathers,* vol. 2, Philip Schaff, ed. (Peabody, Mass.: Henderickson, 1995), 577.

9. Ibid., 578.

10. Ibid., 581.

11. Parker Palmer, *The Courage to Teach* (San Francisco: Jossey-Bass, 1998), 10.

12. Ibid., 11.

13. P. T. Forsyth, *Positive Preaching and Modern Mind* (London: Hodder & Stoughton, 1909), 27.

14. Eugene H. Peterson, *Working the Angles* (Grand Rapids: Eerdmans, 1987), 61.

Chapter 9 Live the Word

1. J. I. Packer, "The Reality Cure," *Christianity Today,* 14 September 1992,

2. Richard Baxter, *The Reformed Pastor* (Portland, Oreg.: Multnomah Press, 1982), 114.

3. Paraphrase of the NIV text: "So that we may present everyone perfect in Christ"; "mature," NRSV; "perfect," KJV; "complete," NASB.

4. C. S. Lewis, *The Problem of Pain* (New York: Macmillan, 1962), 58–59.

5. Søren Kierkegaard, *Works of Love,* translated by Howard Long and Edna Long (New York: Harper & Row, 1962), 123.

6. Dietrich Bonhoeffer, *Life Together,* translated by John Doberstein (New York: Harper & Row, 1954), 26.

7. Ibid., 28.